I Can See Clearly Now

I CAN SEE CLEARLY NOW

How Synchronicity Illuminates Our Lives

Mary Soliel

iUniverse, Inc.
New York Lincoln Shanghai

I Can See Clearly Now

How Synchronicity Illuminates Our Lives

iUniverse books may be ordered through booksellers or by contacting:

iUniverse
2021 Pine Lake Road, Suite 100
Lincoln, NE 68512
www.iuniverse.com
1-800-Authors (1-800-288-4677)

Because of the dynamic nature of the Internet, any Web addresses or links contained in this book may have changed since publication and may no longer be valid.

The views expressed in this work are solely those of the author and do not necessarily reflect the views of the publisher, and the publisher hereby disclaims any responsibility for them.

ISBN: 978-0-595-45860-8 (pbk)
ISBN: 978-0-595-70711-9 (cloth)
ISBN: 978-0-595-90162-3 (ebk)

Printed in the United States of America

This book
is dedicated
with all my love to
my most profound teachers,
my strongest supporters,
my favorite beings,
and
my greatest gifts:

my children.

CONTENTS

~ Author's Note ~

This book is largely an autobiographical work, and all stories are true. To honor their privacy, some names of individuals and a few identifying details have been changed. Also, in recognition of song copyrights, lyrics are referred to in limited form.

Acknowledgments

My heart is filled with love and gratitude for the people in my life who helped with the creation of this book. I thank the following individuals:

Most especially, my dear children, Scott and Karen. You are my absolute bliss. Your extraordinary and unwavering support has been felt and treasured every day. My greatest blessing is to experience life with you beautiful spirit beings.

My magnificent parents, the crème de la crème. You have provided me with constant and unconditional love. You always rooted for me, lifted me up, and made me feel I could accomplish anything. I am so grateful for all that you are.

Julie Libcke, my beautiful and dearest friend for thirty years. You always put up with me, even when I got kooky and New Agey on you. As my first reader, providing advice and encouragement, you are an important part of this work.

Clare Gippo, my wise friend with whom I've shared countless deep discussions. Your brilliance and artistry are an inspiration to me. And your constant faith in me is appreciated.

Elaine Kaiser, my longtime pal since school days. You generously offered so much time to edit and advise, even when you were extremely busy. With your talents and intellect, this proved to be a true blessing for me.

Dr. Deborah Sie, NMD, my mentor. You beautifully graced my life, and my children's lives, with friendship and healing. For that, as well as helping to further reveal the healer in me, my thanks are without end.

Lisa Maeckel, my "Zen" friend. You taught me a gentle and mindful way of being. Thank you for photographing my promotional picture, in front of "Fredericka," the rock.

Cyd, my friend and fellow seeker. Your strength and quest for higher understanding are a testament to the human spirit. I greatly thank you for courageously allowing me to share your story, as it will help so many others.

Cynthia, my writing friend. You mysteriously became a catalyst for the writing of this book with your mere presence.

David, our family friend. Your excitement about this book and desire to preview it meant so much to me.

Gaviota, my "anam cara." You helped me to see and feel beauty in many things.

I also thank all of you whose presence in my life helped me on my path; you know who you are. Thanks also go out to all the strangers and acquaintances who were mirrors for me and helped me to see what I could not on my own.

Mary Mama, my dear grandmother, your spirit presence is golden and deeply felt.

Archangel Michael, our connection is my greatest honor. You have blessed me by shining the light on the Divine part of me, the Divinity we all hold.

I am most deeply grateful to God and the angels who illuminate my life every day and whose guidance and direction have culminated in the writing of this book. You picked me up every time I've fallen and renewed me. I have felt your presence in endless and miraculous ways that constantly fill me with awe and gratitude.

Introduction

One of the world's best-kept secrets is synchronicity. Extraordinary magic is happening everywhere while many of us are in hibernation mode. Our whole Universe is beaming meaningful synchronistic occurrences through our closest relationships, between strangers, in nature—basically all things this earth is made up of—and we are "sleeping" through much of it. We are too busy to recognize what is right before our eyes. When we do awaken to various miraculous signs, we call them "coincidences" and consider them interesting, at most, rather than recognizing them as the Divine gifts they truly are.

I find it puzzling that more of us have not yet embraced the phenomenon, but that is rapidly changing. Synchronicity is accelerating, begging for our attention in these most climactic times, particularly since the dawning of the new millennium, as we are moving quickly toward great change and, ultimately, a more peaceful world. A growing number of people are sensing this Divine intervention and seeking understanding. Living a synchronistic lifestyle is becoming increasingly advantageous as we continue to evolve.

Once you "get it"—that you are receiving, actually attracting, communications from the Universe, constantly and in a myriad of ways—your whole life transforms into a magical, fascinating, and joyful journey. Your most ordinary day can become extraordinary. Signs are not silly and irrelevant, as many would have you believe; they are real and the most precious gifts to be had. There is no such thing as a coincidence.

When you really open yourself up to synchronicity and embrace it, celebrate it, desire it, and live it, you open yourself up to the creation of miracles. You live in a most desirable state of pure Divine connection. Synchronicity can offer your best guidance, validation, and sometimes just the most beautiful winks from Heaven.

Synchronicity exists whether or not we believe in or are aware of its existence. It has to exist. That's the way energy works. We share a multitude of connections with all people, places, and things; everything in life is so intricately and intimately connected. These billions upon billions of connections show up as synchronicities that illuminate our lives so perfectly, so miraculously, so Divinely.

Carl Jung, the Swiss psychiatrist who coined the term *synchronicity*, regarded coincidences as events that defy rational explanations and considered them meaningful, as described in his book *Synchronicity: An Acausal Connecting Principle*. From the time he was a young man, he recognized, in his personal life, that the connection between two or more related events would carry too high a degree of improbability for these events to be labeled as chance occurrences. Dr. Jung eventually witnessed synchronicities experienced by his patients and noted that the wisdom gained from them gave meaning to future events in their lives.

Surprisingly, the word *synchronicity* has not yet found a home in some dictionaries even though the term has been around for decades and was defined by one of the most highly regarded psychiatrists of all time. The inclusion of this Divine word in all dictionaries will mirror the growing awareness of this most grand phenomenon, because the primary criterion for including a word in a dictionary is the frequency with which that word appears in mainstream writing. I would also like to see a new word, *synchronist*, listed as a noun that means "a believer in synchronicity" and "one who studies synchronicity."

The American Heritage Dictionary defines *synchronicity* as a "coincidence of events that seem to be meaningfully related, conceived in Jungian theory as an explanatory principle on the same order as causality," whereas *coincidence* is defined by Dictionary.com Unabridged as "a striking occurrence of two or more events at one time apparently by mere chance," as in, "*Our meeting in Venice was pure coincidence.*"

Some would believe, myself included, that the "meeting in Venice" was in no way a chance occurrence, that no meeting between humans is; that we attract others into our daily experiences on an energetic level and for specific reasons. Could it be that nothing occurs by happenstance? Is it true that we, along with grace and life's mysterious forces, are the growers of the fields of our experiences? Are we creating the most significant aspects down to the minutest details, and chance and luck have nothing to do with this process? Your beliefs regarding these questions deeply affect the way you live and experience life.

Synchronicity taught me that I was creating my reality, and I eventually embraced it as a vital component of my spiritual path. The concept of synchronicity as a phenomenon utilized for conscious creation is explained in the following definition:

"Synchronicities are people, places or events that your soul attracts into your life—to help you evolve or to place emphasis on something going on in your life. The more consciously aware you become of how your soul creates, the higher your frequency goes and the faster your soul manifests. Each day your life will become filled with meaningful coincidences that you have attracted or created in the grid of your experiences in the physical" (*The Center for the New Age Newsletter*, May 2006).

The purpose of this book is to share my personal, spiritual odyssey, along with interpretations of some of life's mysteries learned as a result. Having incubated for twelve years inside of me, this book has poured forth almost effortlessly and at just the right time. All the years I felt stuck and frustrated regarding my purpose has released and unfolded into the very core of why I am here. I believe that I was graced with an abundance of extraordinary synchronicities in my life experience so that they would, indeed, be shared in this very manner.

Some of my stories may seem too unbelievable to be true. Believe me, I am well aware of how karma works, and I have opened my heart with only the purest of integrity here. These stories will open your mind to the grand opportunities and limitless possibilities in your own life. I suggest only that you give synchronicity a chance. Then watch the miracles appear and enjoy the ride. Usually they come through in the gentlest whispers, but sometimes they occur with quite a shout.

The writing of this book has been a hugely synchronistic experience in and of itself. A synchronicity would often guide me first thing in the morning, directing me toward what I would write over those next few hours. Or, on a given day, I would have a clear idea of what specific subject

I would cover, and signs would validate the very points I was making. I describe some of these events throughout the book.

Readers of this book come from all kinds of backgrounds and experiences, and are at varying levels of their conscious spiritual paths. I speak to everyone, knowing that parts of this material might be new concepts to some; to others, it may be just a reminder, or it may be well understood already and even challenged. All of these possibilities are perfect, because we are where we are at this point for a reason.

I deeply respect your beliefs and whatever terms you use to refer to a higher power—*God (He* and/or *She*), *Spirit, the Universe,* et cetera—and I invite you to replace my references with your own. My references to God are made using masculine pronouns, as in *He,* for the ease of expression. Also, I honor your beliefs regarding concepts such as reincarnation and karma. *My hope is that you take only those ideas and concepts described in this book that resonate with you; if they do not, just disregard and take from this read only that which supports your own path.*

My own stories will prompt you to explore how synchronicity has played out in your own life, perhaps without your awareness. For instance, they will cause you to think back to a significant crossroads, when meeting your mate, getting a job you highly desired, or finding a house you loved and felt was perfect for you. You will consider what kind of synchronicity brought you to that point and what miraculous forces came together to help create the event. Your heartfelt acceptance of and gratitude for the synchronicities that have graced your life will not only strengthen your awareness of them but also draw forth more.

Synchronicity brought you to this book for a reason, and I thank you for allowing me to share with you my life experiences and the wisdom I've gained from them. I pray that the following pages will help illuminate your own path and, like ripples in the water, will reach more and more as we further embrace synchronicity into our collective consciousness.

CHAPTER 1

I BEGIN TO REALLY SEE

When I was five years old, I dropped a peeled orange onto the kitchen floor. My mother told me to wash it, but at the same time my dad told me to throw it away. So I washed the orange and then threw it away.

I recall this story with endearment, remembering just how obedient a child I wanted to be for my loving and attentive parents. Hopefully, I knew that my actions didn't make any sense, but I do know I wanted to do what was "right" more than I wanted the orange.

My purpose in sharing this memory is that it reflects my life pattern from a very young age to always do the "right thing," as far as what others believe is acceptable, and to seek validation from outside of myself—to desire approval even if such a desire doesn't make sense. Isn't that what most of us do habitually? We seem to come into this life experience with such tendencies.

We look for validation from not just our parents but also our friends, our spouses, our significant others, our children, our co-workers, our acquaintances, and even strangers. We desire society's approval, because so often our choices and direction in life coincide with what society as a whole believes is right for us even when it may not be right for us individually. We succumb to the pressure to act like everyone else, even when it doesn't feel right to do so.

I am referring to our actions, decisions, and beliefs regarding our relationships, our living spaces, our health, our nutrition, our social behavior, our materialism—in short, everything affecting all aspects of our lives. These endorsed "preferences" then become habitual, and we can find ourselves in a rut of living to please others and society as a whole, which drives us on both conscious and subconscious levels.

We are beginning to understand that some of our choices just aren't working anymore, whether they involve what we do with our lives, what we put into our minds or our bodies, or with whom we choose to spend our time. More of us are feeling a disconnect with many things, and this is causing us to take a deeper look into our life experience. A superficial way of life is no longer sufficient, as more and more of us seek to live more authentically in order to embrace who we really are.

Times are changing as we find that our souls are quietly yet profoundly moving us in a new direction and we, as a collective, spiritually evolve. We are gaining the courage to follow a different "drummer"—ourselves! More specifically, we are pursuing our souls.

In order for us to evolve, we are listening and connecting to our souls' desires and gaining new ground, new possibilities, and new paths on which to venture forth. The old ways aren't working anymore, because we are no longer fulfilled. We are feeling restless for a more profound life experience. We are increasingly uncomfortable when our outside world grows more synthetic and less real. That strong need to conform to others' expectations lessens as the awareness of the nature of our spiritual reality strengthens.

On a deep level, we feel the need to break away from the patterns that have held us back. We are becoming increasingly connected to our higher selves and are seeking spiritually conscious and authentic ways of being. *Ultimately, we are being driven to live from the inside out, rather than the outside in.*

I was nearly thirty-four when I began to discover my new path, my newly preferred way of being. That was when I started to listen and stop looking for validation outside of myself. A most grand teacher brought me this vital awareness. This instructor wasn't in the form of a person. It was synchronicity itself. It was God holding up a mirror that reflected His magnificence in everything from life's most grandiose aspects to its most mundane details.

Synchronicity was illuminating my life, my soul, in every way. It always has and does so for all of us. I just didn't notice. I realized how much of our lives goes unseen: the miracles, the invisible, the mysteries. Hidden, underlying frustrations with the artificial aspects of my existence began to melt away as quickly as they had come into view. This all came with such an undeniable force when I was going through a personal crisis.

Being in the midst of a deep depression caused me to cry out for help. I was on the floor and crying, "Help me! Help me! Help me!" and I would doodle these words over and over again whenever I had a pen in hand. Suddenly, I got help in a big way. God and synchronicity came into my awareness in a profound way that could not be questioned. In this book, I'll focus primarily on the synchronistic aspects of my awakening.

It began in October of 1994, when I lived with my husband and two young children in a suburb of Detroit. At that time, I used to work out in a gym at 5:00 a.m. every morning. One day, when I was on the treadmill, I felt an abrupt interruption in the movement, a jerking of the machine, which caused me to grab on to the side bars, to steady myself, and look at the machine's panel. I noticed that the time I'd spent walking at that point was 11:26, eleven minutes and twenty-six seconds.

Later that morning, I felt the need to look at the (digital) clock, and the time was 11:26. The next day, while on a different treadmill, I experienced the same thing, a jerking motion at the same time, at 11:26! I thought I was losing my mind. Yet this continued to happen on so many occasions that I became convinced that numbers were speaking to me and must absolutely hold great significance and meaning. The Universe definitely wanted to get my attention, and it succeeded.

God was speaking to me, in ways I'd never imagined. I had been spiritually asleep all these years and suddenly woke up, rejoiced, and listened with all my heart and soul. These initial synchronicities caused me to assume *a heightened and relentless awareness of everything in my environment.* They affirmed that magic and meaning are often revealed in the smallest of details, within the most ordinary, seemingly boring aspects of everyday life.

Synchronicities and a deluge of other miraculous experiences coincided with the beginning of my conscious and suddenly illuminated spiritual path. Of course, we're all on spiritual paths, as we are all spiritual beings temporarily inhabiting physical bodies, but nearly thirty-four years passed before I walked the path consciously. Up until this time, I was unaware of the exist-ence of synchronicity.

The connections between events in my life at this time were so pro-found that I did not dare regard them as meaningless coincidences. Read-ing James Redfield's *The Celestine Prophecy* validated my new way of "seeing." I was becoming acutely aware of everything, down to the minu-tiae of my everyday life experiences. For instance, one evening while I was driving in my blue Chevy van, I entertained a negative thought about someone. It wasn't really awful, but, embarrassing to admit, it definitely wasn't nice either.

At the very moment I created the thought in my mind—*bonk!*—I hit an animal. But it wasn't just any animal. It was a skunk, and I immediately realized, as the offensive smell infiltrated my sorry nostrils, that my thought had really "stunk." The awareness of the obvious connection, per-haps along with my sense of smell being overloaded, knocked the wind out of me. The smell even lingered around the garage the next morning, in case I didn't get the message the night before. I felt that this animal gave up its life to teach me a very important lesson, one that would profoundly change my life, so I really wanted to learn it. Our thoughts create our real-ity. They really do.

I also began to enjoy powerful synchronicities in the form of a song, which inspired the title of this book. During my spiritual awakening, so many incredible things happened to me, and I felt "guided" to write about them. The words *I can see clearly now* came into my mind, revealing the title of my future book.

Although I hadn't heard the tune of the same name in a long time, the words seemed to come to me straight from Heaven as the destined title for my book; for the first time in my life, I truly was seeing clearly. That was twelve years ago, but then time does not exist in Heaven. I needed to expe-rience and learn much more before I could attain the wisdom necessary to write my book.

Months later, I was still waiting to hear that song and connect with its lyrics. Of course, iTunes hadn't been invented yet. In January of 1995, I was driving home on a beautiful winter's night in Michigan, watching huge white snowflakes fall from the dark sky onto my windshield and lis-tening to the radio. I've always had a tendency to check the other pro-grammed buttons even after finding a song I like to make sure there isn't a better song playing on another station. If not, I return to the originally picked song.

Well, on this evening I heard the introduction of a song that sounded familiar, an "oldie but goodie." However, I didn't recognize it in those first few bars. I thought the song sounded good, but I decided to see if I could find a better one. I quickly pushed the next button, but the station did not change. When I pushed another button, the station again did not change, so I just let the song play. Never before had my radio buttons failed to respond to my touch. I immediately knew as I felt an unusual pressing sensation in my back that Divine intervention was occurring in my car with my radio. The words began to flow, and I was overjoyed. The song was "I Can See Clearly Now."

This was the first of many synchronicities with a song that immediately became my all-time favorite. It is ageless, beautiful, and utterly inspiring. Have you heard it lately? To me, the song, originally written and sung by Johnny Nash, is about allowing the true magic of life to fill you, being in that bright state of mind no matter what is happening outside of yourself, and thus allowing your life to be illuminated. When we choose to be optimistic while buffering our negative reactions to events in our lives, that single act allows us to live in a more positive light.

Ten days after the first "I Can See Clearly Now" miracle, my little boy and I were listening to the radio while on our way to the grocery store. (By the way, do you get the idea that a lot of synchronicity occurs while driving?) At one point, there was an unusually long pause between songs—just pure silence as if the station had lost its signal—and I had a very strong feeling, an unexplainable confidence, that the next tune would be this very song. Sure enough, as the magical song began to play, I felt tingling sensations on the crown of my head and became filled with an overwhelming sense of awe.

Another ten days later, I felt compelled to turn on the radio at a particular moment, as if I were being directed to do so, and sure enough, the song aired again. I heard that song so many times in that first year and joyfully shared these happenings with my closest friends.

As these extraordinary so-called coincidences were occurring, I was particularly excited to tell my best friend, Julie, about them. One of my favorite synchronicities connected with this song happened nearly six months later while in her presence. At that time, Julie, who loves music, still hadn't heard this song even once on the radio since I'd first shared my experiences with it, and she guessed that it had been years since she'd heard it at all.

It was an early summer evening, and we treated ourselves to a nice dinner at a restaurant on a lake. I was drawn to the deck that overlooked the lake, but Julie wanted to eat inside. My attraction to the deck, as it turned out, had to do with more than the aesthetic enhancement of being seated close to the water.

We went to the deck after dinner but couldn't find anywhere to sit, so we started to leave. However, I felt strangely compelled to stay, and so I led us to another part of the large deck and saw a musician who was getting his guitar ready to perform the first song of his first set. He then began to play "I Can See Clearly Now."

When I told another friend, Elaine, about the synchronicities with this song, she too said she hadn't heard it in years and was amazed that I was hearing it so often. That very evening after I left, her boyfriend came over. They were talking and preparing dinner in her kitchen. At one point, without Elaine having said a word about our conversation, he began to sing to her, "I can see clearly now ..." You will read more about getting nudges from Heaven and saying (or singing, in this case) just the right words at the right time later in the book.

In 1993 Jimmy Cliff recorded a version of the song, which was originally written and recorded by Johnny Nash in 1972, for the soundtrack of the refreshingly unique movie *Cool Runnings*. But this wasn't about being exposed to the hottest hits over and over again. It was about the magic of synchronicity giving me an important message at perfect times through this Heaven-sent song. And music was one of the myriad vehicles for the messages I was receiving.

During those early days of my newfound path, I learned experientially numerous things, spiritual principles really, before I read about them in a book. So, much of what I am sharing with you here was experienced first and then validated through my voracious reading or participation in workshops and conferences, all within the broad subject of spirituality. And I would say to myself, "Well, I knew that." But it wasn't an ego thing; rather it was a validation that what I was reading and learning was true and real, because I'd experienced it first without expectation or previous knowledge.

For instance, one day, again while in my car (See? I told you!), I had the distinct thought that I should buy a lottery ticket and fantasized about receiving a windfall. At that moment, I was parking my car, and another car parked alongside mine. It was a huge red Cadillac, a real estate agent's car. I looked at the magnetic sign on the passenger door, and the words seemed to shoot directly into my brain: EXPECT A MIRACLE!

I get it: *expect* what you desire. "Ask and ye shall receive"—so that's what that means. Except that you must ask with the absolute certainty that you will receive it. There is no room for even an ounce of doubt. No, I didn't win the lottery that week and still haven't, but I learned a valuable concept and a new way of being, thinking, and imagining for life.

Of course, you don't have to be driving in a car to experience synchronicity. That just happens to be one of my most powerful vehicles for receiving signs. As a mom, I'm in the car a lot. However, synchronicities can occur anywhere. We often receive our most meaningful messages while we are at home.

Do you ever wake up with a song running through your head? There surely is a message within those lyrics. Have you ever pondered some issue and then turned on the radio or television just as someone said the words you needed to hear? Have you ever thought of a friend you haven't seen in years, and he or she called you on that very day? Has a coin ever mysteriously and symbolically appeared on your front porch just after you asked to be graced with financial abundance? You probably know that your dreams are among your greatest messengers.

This was how it began for me and is just a brief introduction to the infinite ways that synchronicity can tap you on your shoulder. These initial experiences opened my mind to the understanding of how we create our realities and how we can utilize synchronicity to manifest our greatest desires. They inspired me to look for guidance and validation through my own experiences in the reflection of God's mirror. And they made me see deeper into the life experience, beyond my old "synthetic" ways of thinking and being that society breeds, and passionately choose to live authentically and from the inside out.

Synchronicity illuminates our lives and helps us to see and become who we really are. May the succeeding chapters inspire your own perceptions and may you call forth more of God's magic to fully enlighten your own blessed life.

*   *   *   *

Throughout this book, as I cite examples of synchronicities, please note that my thoughts and feelings that occur in the moment of a synchronistic experience are often connected. They can reveal the meaning. When you remain acutely aware of your thoughts and feelings just as the signs occur, or how the signs in some way coincide with what is going on in your life at the time, you can make the necessary associations. Look for any and all connections. They can provide the key that unlocks the magic.

CHAPTER 2

DOES EVERYTHING
HAPPEN FOR A REASON?

*D*oes everything really happen for a specific reason, or do things occur by accident or chance? The world-altering movie about the Law of Attraction, *The Secret*, tells us that the former is true. Scientists and spiritual teachers featured in the movie *What the BLEEP Do We Know!?* explore the interconnectedness of all things. Albert Einstein said, "At any rate, I am convinced that He (God) does not play dice." What do you believe?

Personal experience, not academics or quantum physicists or spiritual leaders, has absolutely convinced me that we create our life experience, at least on some level. Synchronicity shows me this every day. How can this be a random Universe when miraculous signs constantly shine light on how connected, purposeful, and attracting all aspects of our lives are? These signs cause me to try to understand the reasons behind global events as well as my personal triumphs and struggles. I also believe that just a single incident, however "uneventful," can happen for many reasons, even millions of reasons.

As we seek the truth behind the mysteries of this Universe, understanding the laws that govern it is essential. As presented in Esther and Jerry Hicks's book, *The Law of Attraction*, the most powerful Universal law is indeed the Law of Attraction. "Nothing merely shows up in your experience. *You attract it—all of it. No exceptions.*" It is further explained that because this law "is responding to the thoughts that you hold at all times, it is accurate to say that *you are creating your own reality.*" The Law of Cause and Effect states "that nothing happens by chance or outside the Universal Laws," according to Dr. Norma Milanovich and Dr. Shirley McCune's *The Light Shall Set You Free.*

We are not perfect beings in our human form, but the Law of Attraction, the Law of Cause and Effect, and the many other laws that run the Universe *are* perfect. So why is there so much crisis in the world? The perfect Universe has to act with its perfect laws according to our imperfect free will, "good" and "bad." We cannot blame God for anything, because God is perfection; we are the ones that can mess things up.

I don't claim to be an expert on Universal laws. Rather, I share my story as an expression of my own truth and to continue the dialogue. I believe that our own experiences teach us best. We can be told, taught, and exposed to endless amounts of information from a variety of sources, but when we purposefully participate in a close and relentless observation of our individual realities, therein lies the potential for our greatest wisdom.

The way you live your life depends on whether you believe that this is a deliberate Universe or a random one. I believe it's absolutely vital to address this mystery and consciously decide and then live by your belief. Since my realization back when I hit that skunk that I am indeed creating my reality, I have never gone back to my old ways of thinking. I look closely at the reasons behind most everything, even those boring little details.

Just this morning, I arrived bright and early at my favorite place to write, my local coffee shop, excited to begin working on my laptop. But as I began to set up, I realized I'd left the power cord at home. My absentmindedness reminded me to share an important point. Sometimes a mistake, such as my forgetting to pack the power cord, is the perfect happening. It may allow synchronicity to step in. Specifically, it may cause a particular event to occur or prevent an event from occurring.

We must stop kicking ourselves for our lapses in memory, scolding ourselves for our mistakes, and fretting over our "misfortunes." What if you leave your driver's license in your other purse and miss your plane, but your forgetfulness ends up saving your life because of a doomed flight?

The same goes for quelling our random anger projected at others. What if a slow-moving, preoccupied cashier at the gas station causes you great frustration but actually prevents you from being involved in a pileup on the expressway that happens just seconds before you arrive? There are blessings in disguise everywhere. As I'll point out throughout this book, things aren't always as they seem.

Once you see things from a higher place, you learn to go with the flow of life. You change your attitude about people, situations, and things and adopt a more easygoing and fluid lifestyle that is better for your heart and spirit, not to mention your blood pressure. One of our greatest challenges and most rewarding actions on the spiritual path is to control our reactions to everyday occurrences.

When we control our thoughts and emotions when something "negative" happens and stay reasonably calm, whether reacting to a spouse yelling at us, or someone's poor driving skills, we are creating much better future events. This is a process, and the more you experience and "see" what is really going on, the more easily you can adopt this new attitude toward life.

Having been an emotionally reactive and ultrasensitive personality for as long as I can remember, I've learned and continue to learn to practice healthier and buffered reactions to "negative" events that I believe I have, on some level and in one way or another, actually created.

We are also presented with spiritual tests that, when "passed," propel us further on our paths. The Law of Attraction presents these challenges, which reflect our best opportunities for growth. Some of these tests allow us the chance to react in a more positive manner and thus create and enjoy a more beneficial and peaceful future.

After decades of overreacting, I first got in touch with how unhappy my reactions were making me feel. I was getting very tired of being upset. Then, I became aware of how my reactions were affecting my everyday reality. Whenever something caused a "negative" reaction, it seemed as if that whole day would go wrong. As I began to look for the reasons and the blessings behind the "negative" events, I also learned to observe and modify my own reactions.

When looking at the event from a higher perspective, I would ask myself the following questions: What am I being shown? What would the healthiest response be? What am I feeling? Sometimes the answers were obvious; other times they unfolded as many things happened behind the scenes and for multiple reasons.

If I failed the test and focused on being the victim, I would somehow manifest a new challenge, with similar themes but with new faces, and would get another chance to react favorably. The opportunities would build and magnify until I achieved the understanding and behavior necessary to re-create my life experience. It was synchronicity that delivered and illuminated the gift of experience and the wisdom that resulted from it.

Our life experiences are made up of more than what we create day by day from primarily our thoughts and feelings as well as the spiritual tests with which we are presented. We also come into this world with contractual agreements of our own creation—to be with certain people, to have specific physical or emotional challenges, and so on—for the purpose of our spiritual growth, which will be discussed further in succeeding chapters. Additionally, our reality is made up of the effects of karmic retribution.

Karma refers to the Law of Cause and Effect. What you sow is what you reap. For every good deed you perform, you get back in return. For every bad deed you put out there, you receive in some form as well. It could take a day, a week, a year, or even a lifetime for the karmic retribution to appear. So, if one was hateful toward members of another race, they could return in their next lifetime as a member of that race. But karma has been speeding up over time in our evolution. Its payback can sometimes occur immediately after one's action. Some believe that karma no longer exists. I feel we are moving toward the end of karma as we further embrace the new consciousness.

As I'm writing about karma in the paragraph above, I become aware of the words of a song that is randomly playing on my iTunes via my laptop. I hear "What goes around, comes around ..." I'm thinking to myself, "That's funny. It sounds like she's singing about karma." I look to see what song is playing, and it is literally called "Karma" by Alicia Keys. I didn't know the song well enough to recognize it and had not realized I even had a song of this name. Of the hundreds of shuffled songs that could have been playing while I write this, it was this very one, which synchronistically served to validate the very subject I'm writing about.

The fact is, there truly is a reason behind everything. I see this in my daily life experience. When I get a flat tire, it is always when I'm out of balance. When events or appointments keep getting canceled or are difficult to plan, they are often (not always) wrong for me in the short run or perhaps the long run as well. When anything ails me—back pain, allergies, or low energy—it is always a physical manifestation of what is going on in my life. I create it all, and I've learned over the years to take responsibility for that.

Phew—it's a relief to take responsibility and in any given moment re-create your life's circumstances, especially because you can choose again at any time. Isn't that much better than being subjected to the ramifications of a supposed random Universe?

Oftentimes, an e-mail I'm preparing for someone won't send. I know that when this happens, there is something else I should include or rewrite, because something was unclear or could be misinterpreted. I make the change, and then, sure enough, it sends. It happens every single time.

Every wrong-number phone call I receive happens for a reason. Sometimes these phone calls interrupt what I'm doing or thinking, and then I realize that my attention or thoughts should be elsewhere. Or there may be a specific message in that call. Often the name of the "wrong" caller on my caller ID carries meaning.

The morning after I began reading a book about Mary Magdalene, with whom I've felt an unexplainable connection since I was a little girl, I received a call from "M—Magdaleno," who "accidentally" dialed my number, before 6:00 a.m. no less. Of course, this really got my attention. I left out a few letters for the sake of this person's privacy, but this synchronicity heavily validated my desire to learn more about her.

This happened before I read the hugely popular book *The Da Vinci Code*, by Dan Brown, and witnessed the global surge of interest in Mary Magdalene. And now, a new run of synchronicities regarding her has surfaced, letting me know that the phone call was just the beginning and that I should remain aware.

When I was young and heard the story of Mary Magdalene, I was unsettled to learn that she was a prostitute. I didn't know what a prostitute was, but in my young way of understanding, I knew she wasn't portrayed in a positive light, and I felt it was very wrong.

As children, we have a purer understanding of things; we easily tap into a greater intelligence that is, for most of us, harder to access once we become adults and set up all our rigid beliefs and fears. However, it's never too late to change our minds about anything. We have endless opportunities to do so. Synchronicity will make sure of it, as our souls steer us toward truth.

Sometimes you are involved in the synchronicity, but the message is mostly for someone else. Oftentimes you experience a synchronicity that merely reflects connection from the Heavenly realms. It may not have a profound meaning; it's just a simple and glorious hello. I often look too deeply at things and need to continually remind myself to just stand back and say, "Okay, Mary, don't look so hard at *everything*."

As you tune in to the synchronistic way of living, you become acutely aware of the most "ordinary" events. You are open to the meaning—sometimes heavy, sometimes light—behind even the simplest things. When you board a plane and walk to your seat, whom, through synchronicity, do you find yourself seated next to? What message do you have for that person, or what message does that person have for you? Perhaps it's a quiet ride conducive to your needs, and you don't talk. Or maybe it's a difficult ride with screaming kids or cantankerous adults, which may be a result of karma or negative expectations, or is purely an opportunity to learn patience.

When taking a class, whom are you sitting next to? I have made wonderful new friends and acquaintances just by sitting next to them at a class, meeting, or seminar. Other times I have been challenged by a test or karmic tie with someone I was meant to cross paths with. Allow synchronicity to put you in the right seat with the right people.

So if you are headed toward a comfortable seat with leg room in an auditorium, and someone plows right past you and takes it, synchronicity is probably guiding you to a particular seat next to a particular person. This person may be someone that annoys you, but then what is it within you that needs to be healed? Or he or she may be a good listener, and when the lecturer asks you to share something with the person next to you, you're in the right space for healing, for a show of compassion, or for just being with someone of like mind.

We have the choice to believe that everything occurs by chance or that everything occurs on purpose. Once you see the Universe as a beautifully synchronistic one, there is no going back to the old ways of thinking and being. Nothing will ever be just a coincidence again. Every relationship, every occurrence, every conversation, every mistake, every problem, every joy, every sorrow—each has its own intricate dance, and together they form the dance of the Universe. We are dancing with ourselves, with each other, with nature, with the world, and with God.

CHAPTER 3

NATURE SPEAKS

$\mathcal{N}$othing seems to speak louder than nature. Some of my most significant synchronicities have been presented by birds, rabbits, snakes, coyotes, dogs, insects, rainbows, clouds, feathers, rocks, and water.

Look up any animal in a sign dictionary such as *The Secret Language of Signs*, by Denise Linn, and you will get a clear idea of what the associated sign may mean. For instance, the monkey is a sign "to loosen up and embrace the wild, carefree, mischievous part of yourself." Sometimes, it doesn't matter what type of animal is providing the sign; rather, it is the animal's message that is important, such as when I received confirmation that it was indeed time for this book to be written.

When driving on a quiet road toward Boulder in recent months, I decided and immediately declared that it was finally time to fulfill my destiny. At the exact moment I stated in my mind, "I'm going to write my book about synchronicity," a hawk flew right in front of my car window. Birds had flown close to my car before, but never a hawk. I've always found hawks to be powerful signs, but whenever I spot them, they are flying high or at least perched on a pole or tree; never before (or since) had one swooped down in front of me.

This was undeniable validation that this book needed to be written and that I had the Universe's support. I became filled with gratitude and embraced the firm resolve to move full steam ahead. In this case, the animal's presence relayed the message. The type of animal delivering the sign wasn't as significant, just like when my friend and I were lost in the East Mountains near Albuquerque.

It was dark and late as we drove throughout an isolated area in the mountains, and we couldn't find our friend's home. We were lost, and this was before either of us had a cell phone. So we prayed together out loud and asked for a sign for help in finding our destination. Seconds later, a rabbit darted in front of our car and ran onto a narrow intersecting road ahead of us (that we kept passing by). We immediately regarded this animal as our messenger, so we took that road, and, sure enough, it led us directly to the right place.

When my son and I started reading *Harry Potter and the Sorcerer's Stone*, it was on the eve of the millennium in our new home in New Mexico (we moved from Michigan to New Mexico, and now presently live in Colorado). As you may know, in the first chapter, owls are mentioned several times. After tucking my son into bed, I heard a bird call that I'd never heard before. I went onto our deck, and there, perched above me, was the first owl I'd ever heard making the *whoo-whoo* sounds. Owls are well-known to represent signs of transformation. Of all the nights on which these events could have simultaneously occurred, were a couple hours prior to the new beginning for this world, the first day of the next thousand years.

Before we moved to the Southwest, snakes terrified me. But after we relocated, and knowing we would encounter snakes from time to time, I decided I needed to somehow address my fears and change my perception. It happened in an unexpected way during a visit to a children's science museum.

I did not want to project my own fear onto my children, so when I noticed a group of kids gathering to hold a bull snake, I encouraged my kids to touch it, although I was ready to jump out of my skin. I then forced myself to touch it as well, trying to hide my true feelings. Somehow—and I truly don't remember exactly how it happened—I found myself holding this incredible creature, and I allowed it to move all over me. I truly fell in love with this snake, and my lifelong fear dissolved in a matter of moments. No one could have been more surprised than I was.

Following that experience, we became familiar with a resident bull snake on our land. No, I never picked it up, this one being in the wild and quite large. But, one day, it was waiting for me on our welcome mat. Holding groceries, which I nearly dropped, I spotted it just before nearly stepping on it. A bull snake looks very similar to a rattlesnake, and you need to look at the shape of its head and check whether the tail has a rattle, very quickly in this case, to identify it. After recovering from the surprise, I knew that it had a message for me, especially since it was poised right at the entrance to our home.

Denise Linn's sign book expresses that a snake "is not a sign to be feared." One meaning identified the snake as a symbol for healing. I was about to experience a significant emotional and physical healing at that time. Had I not changed my mind about snakes, I perhaps would not have acknowledged the sign and maybe would have even feared the symbolism or rendered it negative. Perception is everything.

Yesterday, I was shoveling our driveway after all of Colorado experienced a major blizzard that dropped more than two feet of snow. Being outside in the snow filled me with bliss, as I fully enjoyed that peace and quiet that follows a storm. However, my gentle communion with the magical white flakes was interrupted when two birds began to make an unusually loud racket. They got my attention and made me look up. Directly beyond those birds was the only opening to a whitish blue sky on a very cloudy afternoon. And through that slight window past the clouds was the sun. The winter solstice was only hours away, and I needed to recognize it.

As I sit in my favorite coffee shop writing the paragraph above, the man at the next table is telling a story about "two birds." How often do people speak or write about "two birds"? Now, don't think I'm in the habit of honing in on other people's conversations, but when this kind of synchronicity happens, I cannot help but hear. I feel that I automatically tune in, as voices seem raised when I need to be aware. See how connected we really are? Nothing has ever personally felt so Divinely inspired and guided as the writing of this book. Imagine getting this kind of validation when you live your purpose, because it is there.

Earlier that same morning, I watched the local news, which I rarely do; I wanted to find out about the blizzard's aftereffects and the forecast. The second I turned it on, the anchorman said, "And look at this picture of the sun." And it was a phenomenal view of the sun on the solstice. I need to be aware of the solstices and equinoxes, because they are always powerful and transformative. When I forget, synchronicity will step in to remind me.

Do you think that those in the Heavenly realms can give you clear and direct messages by writing them in the sky? Clouds are one of my favorite signs. I believe they speak volumes—such as the time I flew to Denver and then took a van from the airport with nearly a dozen people on the way to Breckenridge to attend a spiritual conference. We all were stunned to see a magnificent stream of clouds that together perfectly formed an image of an angel with arms spread wide open as if welcoming us. When we arrived at our destination, we saw that the theme of the conference had to do with angels, and the promotional signs, badges, and programs all featured an image of a beautiful angel.

An unforgettable sighting of a cloud occurred when I once felt Jesus's presence with me and heard in my mind the words "anchor in My love." Just then, I looked up and saw a cloud perfectly shaped like an anchor, and it then dissipated very quickly. It was a deeply profound experience.

After attending a financial abundance seminar—and after having just seen the movie *The Secret*, which features Aladdin's lamp in some segments—I saw a cloud that looked exactly, to my great shock, like the genie's lamp. This spoke to me the message, "Your wish is my command." How's that for validation?

Signs, such as a rainbow, appear just when you need them. If you suddenly spot a rainbow when you weren't even looking for one after a storm, you were probably being nudged to notice. When you see a rainbow, or a cloud shaped like a feather, angel wing, or even an exclamation point as I have on occasion, consider what is going on in your life or what thoughts you are holding in that moment, because you may be receiving a grand validation.

I had never seen a cloud that even vaguely resembled an anchor, or Aladdin's lamp for that matter, until these specific, perfectly timed occurrences.

As I'm writing this, a woman near me loudly proclaimed, "There is a God!" in an animated conversation with her friends.

Oh yes, there is. And He speaks to all of us all the time, through clouds, animals, strangers, families, and friends. He speaks to us through the song on the radio, the shadow on the sidewalk, and the feather blowing in the wind. He speaks to us in our dreams and meditations. And so very often, our hearts are spoken to directly. We are always being given messages from God and from Heaven. We need only believe it and listen, with our ears, eyes, and feelings.

The song that began playing on my iTunes (which is always set to shuffle mode so that songs are played in random order) as I wrote the last sentence of the paragraph above was "Listen," gorgeously sung by Beyoncé in the movie Dreamgirls. *So allow me to put special emphasis on the word "listen."*

Months after writing this chapter, I'm now rereading it for editorial purposes, and, again, the song "Listen" came on as I reread this same paragraph! As the song says, you must start listening "to the sound from deep within." Obviously, this message is being synchronistically emphasized for you, the reader.

Water is a beautiful and powerful visual sign; and it even asserts itself in unseen ways. When I practiced hypnotherapy, I shared with every new client the visionary Masaru Emoto's book, *Messages from Water.* Dr. Emoto took pictures of frozen water crystals after the water had been exposed to various words, pictures, or music. His research proved that the same distilled control water was changed and affected by each stimulus. For example, water exposed to the word *love* produced a beautiful, well-formed crystal, whereas a crystal formed after exposure to the words *you fool* was unattractive and erratically formed.

These experiments dramatically show that water responds to the energetic vibration of what it is exposed to. Our bodies contain roughly 70 percent water. Doesn't this mean that basically everything in our awareness is affecting the water in our bodies, whether positively or negatively? This includes most especially our thoughts, our feelings, what we say, and what we do—specifically, the music we listen to, the television shows we watch, the news we expose ourselves to, and the people we spend time with, because there is energy in all things, and we are responding to it all.

Through Dr. Emoto's book, I attained visual proof of what I already believed—that everything we think, feel, say, and do affects our reality.

After seeing the frozen water crystal photos for the first time, I began writing positive and loving words right onto my water bottles and suggested to my clients that they do the same.

My personal experience with water (or any liquid) is that whenever I spill it on myself, it is something to be blessed, and not cursed for clumsiness. It is a sign that my cup will overflow with abundance of some kind. My first awareness of the meaning behind water spilling happened in Las Vegas of all places.

I met my parents and brother in the City of Lights, and although we were having a great time together, I kept losing. I was down to the last $40 I'd set aside to gamble with and began playing at a roulette table. Because I was immediately starting to lose, I told the dealer, "Color in," which means "I want to cash in." She said, "Are you sure you want to leave so early?" I had a feeling that she "knew" something I didn't, so I decided to continue playing. I was particularly enamored with playing the double digits—11, 22, 33, and 00—on each spin.

Just as she spun the ball inside the wheel, a man knocked over his drink. Okay, it probably held something other than water, but the spilled liquid made a perfect beeline toward me at the end of the table. I instinctively felt that this was a good sign. Sure enough, 11 came in. I built up my bets, and 11 came in again. I piled up my bets like never before, and 22 came in. I left the table with $2,200, more than I had ever won. I intuited, during these exciting moments, that there was a link between water spilling and the presence of good fortune. I went to another casino and grossed another $1,500. It seemed as if I couldn't lose, but I needed to leave for my flight home.

The abundance heightened on the plane when I met a man with a beautiful spirit who happened to be a pastor at a church in Albuquerque. During the course of our conversation, I mentioned that it was my greatest hope that our recent move to New Mexico would help my son's asthma condition. He invited me to his church, and a few weeks later we did indeed attend as a family.

We were the only Caucasians attending this African American parish. We had never felt more welcome anywhere than we did in this small church with a huge heart; nearly every parishioner in the congregation went out of his or her way to meet us, shake our hands, or hug us. I was deeply touched by such an unusual display of warmth and kindness from people we'd never met. I remember thinking to myself that if everyone treated each other like this, our world would change in the blink of an eye.

Following the conclusion of the service, the pastor did a very special and dramatic healing on my son. Ever since that day, Scott has been off of his daily asthma medications. The synchronicity of being seated next to this man on that one flight brought us together for a blessed purpose.

Water signs continued years later when I attended that financial abundance seminar in Denver. We broke for lunch, and I went with a friend to a very busy pizza place. I was holding a tray with a glass of water, waiting for a slice of pizza, and a man bumped very hard into me, causing the water to spill all over my blouse, including my conference badge. My initial reaction wasn't one of joy, but as soon as I realized that it was actually a blessing and a sign, a smile spread across my face. Again, I connected the spill of water to good fortune, especially because I was in the mode of learning about attaining wealth.

When returning home, two city workers were releasing water from the fire hydrant across the street from my house. The water was gushing directly onto our front lawn. Had that happened any other time, I might not have thought much of it, but having just attended this conference about gaining financial freedom, I saw particular relevance in the timing of water spilling onto my property. Just a few days later, I found almost $1.00 in coins on our lawn—another symbol of abundance.

Whenever I see people spill water or any liquid on themselves, I say to them, "It's a good sign." They probably think I'm just trying to make them feel better or less embarrassed, but my sentiments are genuinely expressed. Most seem surprised at the idea that it would represent a positive personal sign for them.

I join in the belief that we are in the age of abundance—abundance of joy, peace, love, health, money, et cetera. We're being told this by a multitude of messengers, healers, visionaries, and teachers. As will be described further in this book, we are being taught to consciously create that which we desire. When we allow synchronicity to carve the path to conscious creation, so often through all the miraculous aspects of nature, we indeed make our dreams come true.

Nature entices us with its most awesome signs, to draw us out of our homes and busy lives in order to connect with the real earth. It inspires us to commune with the miracles in our everyday existence, even if it involves nothing more than noticing a ladybug crawling up your arm or taking a moment to look upward at the clouds in the sky. As Mahatma Gandhi said, "When I admire the wonders of a sunset or the beauty of the moon, my soul expands in worship of the Creator."

CHAPTER 4

THE CHIHUAHUA PRESENCE

Sometimes signs are purely an unfolding. You may need days, weeks, months, or even years to fully understand what they mean, and, thus, patience is required. They are a peek into the future with a display of a potential occurrence, path, or understanding. An absolutely stunning thread of synchronicities is still unfolding in my life.

On January 10, 2001, I decided to treat myself with a visit to a bookstore. I bought a novel called *The Saving Graces*. I hadn't read anything but spiritual publications for years but felt strangely compelled to purchase this book. After leaving the store, I drove to "Old Town" for some authentic southwestern food. Old Town is located not far from what New Mexicans call "The Big I," where the state's main expressways, I-40 and I-25, intersect. At that time, this intersection was undergoing a major renovation.

Following a quick meal, I headed for home, merging onto the expressway to go eastbound on I-40 toward The Big I. My car started to sound strange. I kept pushing on the gas pedal but could not achieve a steady rate of acceleration, and I suddenly realized what was happening. For the first time in my life, I was running out of gas, with nowhere to go. Because of the major road reconstruction, cement barricades lined the lanes, which prevented the shoulder from "saving" me.

I thanked God out loud when I saw an exit about an eighth of a mile down. There was a gas station ahead, and I would be just able to sputter my way to the exit. However, the exit ramp was barricaded as well. I started praying very hard and very loudly; my car moved incrementally with every few pushes on the gas pedal while cars and semis rushed past me.

Although my car seemed to be running on fumes at this point, I some-how made it safely to where the shoulder reopens for the southbound approach onto I-25, right at the main intersection—The Big I. While intensely thanking God for keeping me safe, I put my car into park. At that moment, a truck with a huge picture of Christ on the cross went past me. A truck with a picture of Christ on it? I couldn't believe this but had no time to think about it, because suddenly several horns started to sound, and I heard brakes screeching behind me.

Was I going to get hit? What was going on now? I looked in my side-view mirror and could not believe my eyes. A little Chihuahua was running along the same path I'd just driven toward The Big I! Here was this tiny dog right in the midst of the biggest interchange in all of New Mexico. Terrified, it was desperately trying to find safety as drivers slammed on their brakes to avoid hitting it.

I immediately got out of my car to save it, as it ran toward where I was parked. Being so scared, it didn't realize I was trying to help it, and to my horror, it started to go into the road. I immediately grabbed it, and at that moment, it bit me out of fear. During this time, I was vaguely aware that a police car had been parked about one hundred feet or so ahead of me. The officers just sat in the car while I played hero, but I later realized that I was the one who needed to save this little Chihuahua.

With feelings of great relief, I took the dog over to the policemen, showed them that it had no tag, and then offered to take it to the animal shelter. They wanted to take it themselves, but it was hard for me to let them. I felt a connection to this tiny white, brown, and black being that somehow survived The Big I. How on earth did a little dog like this get onto the expressway? I wanted to be sure it would be okay after all it had endured. (As it turned out, it was quarantined for a few days, and on the morning that it was to be put up for adoption, it was selected and taken just ten minutes after the shelter opened.)

After the policemen took the Chihuahua, I called AAA, and they came with a gallon of gas. I wanted to fill up right away, vowing to never again drive on a sparsely filled tank, and went to a nearby gas station. I pumped some gas and then called my husband, on my cell phone, to tell him what had happened.

As I drove down a side street, explaining to Jack the astonishing occurrence with the Chihuahua, *another* Chihuahua walked right in front of my car! I was screaming into the phone, telling Jack about this light brown Chihuahua that just crossed the street directly in front of me. Aren't they lapdogs, people dogs, which are rarely outside on their own and certainly never far from their owners?

I'm sure my poor husband's ears did not appreciate my screams of shock. He, being used to my synchronistic experiences and my yearning to find meanings in each of them, said playfully, "I think it means you need to go to Taco Bell." He was referring to the Taco Bell commercials that featured their popular Chihuahua mascot. I knew that the message here was much more significant than that. The Universe had gone through a lot of trouble to synchronize these amazing events. What I didn't know then was that this was just the beginning and that the meaning of these events would unfold over several years.

The synchronicities continued through the day. I began reading *The Saving Graces*—the book I had bought that morning. The first chapter described how four women friends *save a dog*! Later in the book, one character learns that she has breast cancer; as I was literally reading this section, we received a phone call. It was from a relative of ours, who told us that she'd just found out that she has breast cancer (thankfully, she fully recovered following treatment). This was overwhelming. I felt confused, and I yearned for clarity and understanding.

Months later, I was driving down Central Avenue toward the University of New Mexico, and a black Chihuahua stopped four busy lanes of traffic just one car ahead of me and safely made it to the other side. I happened to notice that the time was 11:11 a.m. (the significance of which is explained in the following chapter). But even that could not prepare me for one of the most incredible, most awe-inspiring synchronicities of my life that rivaled, yet perfectly mirrored, The Big I experience.

We lived in the desert, which consisted mostly of dirt, rocks, junipers, and cacti, in an area with homes that were separated by at least an acre. Situated in the foothills of the Sandia Mountains, the area was very hilly, and our mailbox was a half mile from our house. One day, my young son asked to make the climb up, between the homes, to the mailbox. He had never hiked to the mailbox before. Being the ever-protective mom, and because we did live among snakes and other wonders, I asked him to take his walkie-talkie along.

At one point in his journey, he used his walkie-talkie to tell me that he'd found some mail. It hadn't been in the mailbox; he'd found it lying in the dirt between two homes halfway up. I told him to bring it home and that we'd get it to the right person. When he returned, I saw that there was no address on the envelope, only the name "Larry," and it appeared to contain a greeting card. It looked as if it had been on the ground for months, soaked with rain, and then dried; it was quite warped but still sealed.

I didn't know of a man named Larry. Given that winds sometimes surpass fifty miles per hour in our area, the envelope could have been blown a great distance. I called several neighbors to ask if they knew of a Larry, but no one else did either. One woman told me to open the envelope, because the contents may provide a clue. So with my kids there, I opened it. Indeed, it was a greeting card.

On the front of it was a picture of a Chihuahua. Above the dog was an image of an eyeball—a very strange-looking card. It was my very wise and intuitive seven-year-old daughter, Karen, who figured it out right away: "Mom, it's a big eye! You know, the Chihuahua and The Big I!" *Wow.* Can you imagine how we felt as we looked at the picture and began to understand? We couldn't believe it. Inside the card were the words "Ay, Chihuahua! You're how old?" It was a birthday card (see photo). To top it off, it was signed by "Scott," the name of my son. And here it was Scott, himself, who suddenly desired to hike this path which led him to finding the card with a miraculous message. All three of us hugged each other; always celebrating these incredible occurrences.

The Chihuahua synchronicities continued. Years later, a Chihuahua again walked in front of my car in a subdivision in Colorado. Yet another time, while entertaining friends from out of town, we all took our dogs for a walk. We arrived at a park, and a girl came up to me and said that her little sister wanted to pet my dog, a mixed Labrador retriever. She said that her sister is usually scared of dogs, mostly Chihuahuas. I intuited that this was a sign that I should tell my friends about my most treasured synchronicities, which I had been wanting to share with them.

The next morning, I picked up my friend who lived a few blocks away to go for a walk. Among the very first words out of her mouth were, "Ay, Chihuahua!"—the saying on the greeting card! Now, I never hear people use this phrase. I knew that, again, I was getting a sign to tell this friend, too.

As I edit this chapter, I realize that all three of the people described in the two paragraphs above are healers like myself. This helps with deciphering the meaning behind the Chihuahua synchronicities.

The day after that, while driving toward home, I heard in my mind the words, "Go down here," on a street that was not normally on my way home but was on the way to the aforementioned friend's home. Just two houses away from her house, I saw a woman from the back, tall with long brown hair, and I thought this person was my friend. It turned out she wasn't, but this lady was walking her dog, which just happened to be a Chihuahua.

I recently dreamed that I had a Chihuahua. It was golden brown, and I absolutely loved it. Upon waking and recalling the dream, I thought that if I ever got a Chihuahua, I'd like a golden one. When I went to my computer that morning, to my home page, which always shows the three most e-mailed photos, two out of the three pictures were of golden Chihuahuas.

The funny thing is, I was never a fan of the breed, but now I am. However, the meaning goes much deeper than wanting to have one as a pet. My most recent Chihuahua synchronicity occurred just a week ago. I was driving my son to school, and as we approached an intersection, I was experiencing synchronicities that somewhat mirrored The Big I experience—subtle but vivid enough to permit recollection—and just then my son said, "Look, Mom ... a Chihuahua." And sure enough, in the car next to ours was a Chihuahua standing on its owner's lap. "Hmmm," I thought. "Things are cooking again."

All this can mean so many things. It truly is an unfolding. Once I had a friend who at one point felt quite terrified, just like the dog at The Big I, and when I reached out and helped her, she "bit" me. Is it about that? Is it that I will be "saved"? Is it that I will help "save" others through writing, teaching, healing, and speaking? Is it about all these things, because even just one synchronicity often holds many meanings? It appears it is mostly about salvation, healing, and grace as I continue to seek further clarity on my path.

CHAPTER 5

NUMBERS, NUMBERS, NUMBERS

Okay, I'm ready to admit something to you. I'm … I'm a … all right, here it goes. I am a … number maniac—an absolute number freak! I love numbers. I cannot get enough of them. I look for them everywhere, and I am often convinced they are looking for me. On clocks, addresses, store receipts, phone numbers, signage, trucks, the Internet, and even license plates, I notice them. When the same numbers are repeated in double or triplicate, I get really excited. And then I want more. Do you think I'm strange? I certainly did, in the beginning, but I eventually learned about the science of numbers, and as the years passed, I met others who were crazy about numbers just like me, people who were aware of numbers' significant meanings.

Numbers are the true universal language. Go to any country in the world, and you may not be able to speak the same language, but you can relate in numbers. Everything comes down to numbers, absolutely everything. A person, a table, a watermelon, an airplane, a fossil, a cloud—they all come down to numbers. Numbers carry energy, and they are full of meaning. They burst with meaning. So consider yourself forewarned of my magnificent obsession.

You may recall the synchronicities with 11:26 that I explained in the first chapter "I Begin to Really See." That sparked my twelve-year (and ongoing) search for the meaning behind these wonderful digits. It's as if there is some aura around them; they are highlighted within my sight, and they beg for my attention as much as I pursue them.

I was actually relieved to learn about numerology, the study of numbers, because it made me feel a little less weird. Yes, an actual science to my preoccupation existed, and I soon learned that meanings are assigned to numbers. Although I've incorporated the formal meanings of specific numbers into my own assessments of numbers, I also use my personal intuitions on what certain numbers mean to me.

Just yesterday, when driving, I saw two cars right in front of me, traveling side by side, both with 111 on the license plates. They drove the same speed, staying perfectly together, so I was easily able to notice. The number 1, in triplicate especially, is known to symbolize new beginnings. Think of the chances of that happening. The odds of seeing just one license plate with 111 along with any one set of letters (such as 111XYZ) are roughly one in a thousand, and I saw two right in line with each other. I am experiencing a new beginning right now with the writing of this book, and seeing these cars together emphasized that message. And during these past few weeks, many 111s have been in my awareness.

A few months down the road, I may get a sudden rash of more 111s, which could signify other new beginnings, perhaps meeting a soul mate or experiencing a spiritual advancement. We all have—or, I should say, create—many new beginnings throughout our lives. Even when I'm in my later years, I'm sure I will continue to see and be shown 111 signs. With new beginnings, we keep growing and learning, something we hopefully never stop doing.

My life-destiny number, according to numerology, is an 8. You can calculate your life-destiny number by adding up all the digits of your birth date: the month, day, and year. For instance, if you were born on January 6, 1960, you would compute 1 + 6 + 1 + 9 + 6 + 0, which totals 23. Then, you would add the digits 2 and 3, which equals 5. Dan Millman's *The Life You Were Born to Live: A Guide to Finding Your Life Purpose* is an excellent resource for discovering meanings of birth numbers and how they relate to your life path.

Because my birth date adds up to a 26, I add 2 and 6 and get an 8. The number 8 has to do with abundance and power. The 8 on its side symbolizes infinity. People who are 8s are here to deal primarily with issues concerning money and power, whether the lack or abundance of it. It wasn't until this past year that I began to focus on attaining financial freedom. Being a single mom with new responsibilities has forced me to confront the negative beliefs I've held about money not only since childhood, when we all form most of our misbeliefs, but also from past lifetimes.

When you see the same number doubled or in triplicate, the meaning is clearly more significant. How many of you are catching 1:11, 2:22, 3:33, 4:44, 5:55, 10:10, 11:11, or 12:12 on your clock? Come on, admit it. What about 1:23, 12:34, or 7:11? Yes? That's fabulous. If you haven't, I bet you will start noticing soon. But you won't necessarily be noticing on your own. Your angels will be giving you a nudge, getting you to look at the clock at just the right moment. The first couple of times it occurs may not feel so significant, but when it keeps happening, you will most likely pay close attention, and it will truly make you giggle.

I no longer use a microwave because of potentially negative effects on health, but when I did, if the food or drink needed a minute-long zap, I would always set the timer for 1:11. Or if it required five minutes, I'd set the timer for 4:44. I sound like an obsessive-compulsive, eh? Although I admit to having some OCD tendencies, this was more of a celebratory practice. I would laugh at myself for this strange behavior, but I couldn't help myself. "Now *this* is weird, Mary!" I'd say to myself.

When present at a spiritual conference, and when it was shared, with a dose of humor, that one of the main speakers never puts just one minute on the microwave but has to set the timer for 1:11, I knew I was not alone. Many of us are tuned in to numbers. They are one of the many ways that Heaven connects to us in a synchronistic way in order to guide, validate, and often just amuse and remind us that we are in excellent company at all times.

My favorite set of numbers is 444. It became so after reading Nick Bunick's autobiography *In God's Truth*, and the biography *The Messengers*. Without giving away his incredible story, he refers to 444 as being the angels' sign of "the power of God's love." Ever since reading about that, 444s have become blissful messengers for me.

If you start waking up at 4:44 a.m., I guarantee that your angels are waking you, just for you to take notice. In fact, if these concepts are new to you, I am convinced that with your newfound awareness of 444, or any numbers in triplicate, with your angels completely knowing this, you will enjoy an abundance of 444s and other number synchronicities in your life. As I write this, I feel that the angels are excited and planning to make you truly aware of their presence in your life and to remind you that the power of God's love is always with you. You'll see.

My friend, Cynthia, read a draft of this book. The very next morning after having read this chapter, she woke up at 4:44 a.m.! I'd never told her about the 444 phenomenon, so she'd learned about it from this book. Cynthia told me she is an excellent sleeper and hardly ever wakes up early. When she has on very rare occasions, she said she goes right back to sleep without looking at the clock. However, on this night, she was nudged to look, and it was 4:44! Thanks, angels. I knew you'd come through!

Having experienced many 444 signs over the years, I was driving in Santa Fe, known to some as the "City of Synchronicity." Visits to this city nearly always proved to be highly synchronistic experiences for me. On this particular day, within a span of just one mile, I saw three cars with 444 on the license plates. Again, the chance of seeing just one 444 with any combination of letters is roughly one in a thousand, and I saw three so close together.

That night, my kids, my husband, and I went out to dinner at our favorite restaurant near our home. I told them about seeing three cars with 444s within a mile's distance. After telling them, we got the bill. It was for $44.40! It wasn't even our bill, but it needed to "mistakenly" reach our table to make a point at the most perfect time. The angels had our undivided attention. They presented the most beautiful reminder that the power of God's love is with us. It so perfectly validated and magnified my 444 experiences earlier that day.

I remember telling my friend, Kat, that I wished my car's New Mexico license plate read 444 and was considering getting a personalized plate with those numbers. That way, I explained, my car would be spreading the 444 message and energy that Nick Bunick first brought to the world, wherever I would drive. She too was absorbed with the meanings of numbers, so she asked what my license plate did read. I said it was "700MDM." Kat said, "That *is* 444!" Every letter in the alphabet has a numerical vibration associated with it, and both *M* and *D*, as well as *V*, are 4s (a numerology chart can be found at the end of this chapter). Even though I was well aware that letters carry numerical vibrations, all that time I was driving around with the 444 energy, without even realizing it.

When I went to the bookstore recently to pick up a paperback for my daughter, I quickly perused the metaphysical section. I noticed a book that included a foreword by Nick Bunick, so I read his message and then purchased Karen's book. When I returned to my car just minutes later and began to back out of the parking space, I saw that the car parked in front of me had a 444 license plate. It wasn't there when I initially parked the car. Oh, and by the way, the book purchase came to $7.77.

This morning, after driving my son to school, I saw a stunning sunrise; the sun looked huge, blazing with a gorgeous red and beautifully reflecting on the lake by our home. I saw it for only a split second, because houses soon blocked the view, but it was an awesome sight. As soon as I put my eyes back on the road, I noticed that the red sports car next to me had a 444 license plate, and I saw it in just enough time to make my turn into the subdivision. Again, when I plan ahead to write about a particular subject on any given day, it is often validated through synchronicity.

As I was thinking about what more I could share in this chapter, I recalled the time when the odometer on my Jeep read 44,444 miles, and at that exact moment, a car passed me with a 444 license plate. Just as I entertained this memory when picking up my son from school, I heard the person on a radio ad promoting car service ask, "Have you checked your odometer lately?" Well, yes, I have to admit that I do check my odometer—quite often, in fact.

Sometimes I have been nudged awake at 4:43 a.m. and know the angels are playing a little joke on me. I've realized from many occasions that humor is big in the other realms, and I love laughing along with my angels. They remind me not to take life so seriously, a reminder I need quite often. This happened again just a few days ago when I woke up with a good laugh at 4:43. The very next morning, I was woken at 4:44! I have a friend who has awakened at 2:22, gone back to sleep, and then reawakened at 4:44, and when this happens, she knows the angels are *really* trying to get her attention.

This same friend, Clare, has her own special number that holds great personal meaning. When she was a little girl, she used to tell her father all the time, "I love you 712!" At that time, she felt that 712 was the biggest number she could count up to, and so that was her way of expressing how much she loved him. They continued throughout her childhood and even adulthood to say, "I love you 712!" to each other, until his death several years ago.

Since her father's transition to Heaven, Clare sees the number 712 so often and at the most meaningful times, and she knows without a doubt it's her father saying, "I love you 712!" She regularly wakes up naturally at 7:12, and the change she receives from a purchase at a store will oftentimes be $7.12.

Recently, when earnestly paying her bills, she checked to see how much money was left in her account to make sure she had enough to cover her last check. The calculator showed $71.2, as her calculator never shows a zero in the hundredth column. Clare said she laughed out loud when that happened; she was sure that it was her dad saying, "Lighten up! Don't worry! Everything's going to be okay."

As mentioned before, there are formal interpretations of numbers. From my experience, I have found that 1 means new beginnings, as well as creativity, 2 denotes the balance of opposites, 3 relates to expression, 4 is security, 5 cues good, surprising change and freedom, 6 mirrors harmony, 7 calls for endings leading to new beginnings, 8 represents money and power, 9 signals completion, and 0 reflects spiritual gifts. I'm particularly enamored with the powerful master numbers 11, 22, and 33. Number 11 is known to stand for illumination, whereas 22 refers to a master builder. The number 33 means master teacher, and has been considered to reflect the message, "With God, all things are possible," a most beautiful numerical meaning.

More and more people are catching 11:11 repeatedly on their clocks, and this phenomenon is known to reflect humanity's collective permission to change the course of earth toward peace, instead of prophesized destruction. Many believe it's a wake-up call, a reminder that says we're on the track to earth's new reality. This connection most resonates with me. However, the meaning should be ultimately left to the individual. I've heard many different interpretations of this number combination. Some simply regard it as good luck and make wishes when they notice it.

I, like Clare, have attached my own personal meanings to certain numbers, especially when I've associated a number with a person or an experience, and of course the angels, as well as our passed loved ones, are very aware of just what these associations are. Clare's story is a perfect and most endearing example of that.

It felt as if the angels were preparing me for something a few months ago. As I pulled into a gas station, I noticed that on the other side of the pump was a car with a 444 license plate. A woman dressed in a surgical uniform emerged from the car. I intuited that a medical situation of some sort was going to present itself that day, but all was going to be fine. When I arrived at a meeting that morning, I happened to notice a woman wearing a blouse with a leopard design, black slacks, and leopard shoes. It's unusual for me to take notice of fashion. I am always more interested in whom I'm talking to and what they have to say, rather than what they are wearing, but the woman's fashion coordination did register with me.

When I picked up my daughter from school later that day, she said that she'd experienced a strange visual disturbance during her last class, where she could not see anything directly in front of her, and that things were still somewhat blurry. I took her straight to the eye doctor and was able to get her checked out right away. Normally, I would have gone into a major state of worry over a situation such as this and would have struggled to hide my fear. Instead, I felt so calm inside. I knew that everything was going to be okay.

The technician called us into the exam room, and I was amazed to see what she was wearing—a leopard top, black slacks, and leopard shoes. Now how often do you see women wearing this combination? She wasn't the same person I'd seen at the meeting; however, she represented a sign that this was all predestined. The events of the day blessed me with, well, let's call it an intuitive preview.

As it turned out, there was nothing to be concerned about; the doctor assured us that, to my surprise, people do experience this from time to time. Since childhood, I've had a tendency to panic about things, overreact, and worry. I came in wired that way, but this time I held a calm demeanor—thanks to the signs.

A student of mine was so intrigued by my 444 synchronicities, some of which I shared in my "Become a Conscious Creator" class, that she immediately began having them herself. While driving, she asked for a sign that her young son would have a successful acting audition. Just then, a purple taxicab displaying the phone number 444-4444 drove by. When she asked about her daughter's audition, nothing distinguishable occurred. As it turned out, her son got the part, and her daughter didn't.

Many people use numbers to determine important life decisions; when purchasing a house, for example, they will consider the address and add up the numbers. When we lived in New Mexico, our house number was 49. When you add 4 and 9, you of course get 13, and if you add 1 and 3, you get 4. A four home is known to be a secure home, inhabited with an orderly manner. We are now temporarily living in an eight home, as I'm learning to choose new thoughts and beliefs about money and abundance.

Every year carries a numerical energy. The year 2007 carried the energy of 9, by adding 2 + 0 + 0 + 7, which represents completion. On the other hand, 2008 is a one year (2 + 0 + 0 + 8 = 10, 1 + 0 = 1), which signifies new beginnings. This can be seen on personal and even global levels.

On a personal level, 2007 will be regarded by many, myself included, as a year filled with great challenge, sometimes overwhelming difficulties, and welcome endings, whereas 2008 holds the promise of a new start in many aspects of our lives.

As I complete the final edit of this book, I realize that this explains, from a higher perspective, why various events and last minute additions caused me to delay the publishing of this book until early 2008. It is all Divine.

Looking at American politics, 2007 reflects a year of completion in the ending of the way things were in the political arena. The shift in Congress, which moved to a Democratic majority in the House and Senate, represents a completion of the Republicans' domination. In 2008, many new beginnings will likely surface in a year of political change culminating with elections.

Always use discernment when deciding what synchronicities mean, including those with numbers. When I was thinking about getting a lottery ticket, at that very moment, I saw a license plate that read "888MNY." I couldn't get to the lottery ticket vendor quick enough. Did I then win, or have I ever won, the lottery? No. Am I being reminded still to "expect a miracle"? Yes. I always intend to be graced with miracles. It may be unlikely that my financial abundance will come through the lottery, but the point is, I'm choosing to take actions that communicate to the Universe, in many different ways, that I am serious in my desire to create the financial means that allows me to fulfill my destined purpose as an author, teacher, and healer. I know that anything is possible.

It is important to surrender to the manner in which abundance will come forth. The Universe will take care of that. And then it is your responsibility to act on it. Your intentions must come from thoughts of abundance, not feelings of lack. In the case of money, if it doesn't come when you expect it to, what is your reaction? Always stay vigilant of your thoughts and how you react. Focus on what you do have, what you appreciate in your life in this moment, so you can breed more and more of it. Whether you have $100 or $1 million in your bank account, if you feel gratitude for that money, your focus on it can attract more.

What we focus on expands, whether in a positive or a negative way. I'm not at all a sports fan, but I was aware that when my alma mater, the University of Michigan, played Ohio State in November of 2006, it was a big deciding game. Ohio State won 42 to 39. After the game, with millions focused on the final score, the four numbers picked for Ohio's four-number state lottery were 4, 2, 3, and 9.

Whether the focus is one of celebration or tragedy, it manifests in the real world. On the first anniversary of 9/11—that is, September 11, 2002—the three-number lottery pick in New York City was 9, 1, and 1, in that order, and thousands of people actually picked that sequence of numbers.

When the Universe, the angels, and departed loved ones shower you with messages through numbers, look at the patterns and decipher the meanings for yourself. You may find yourself mostly surrounded by the energy of 1s, of new beginnings, or 5s, the energy of change, during a certain period of time. Then the numerical energy will shift as your life circumstances and potentials shift. Remember, you don't always have to delve deep into symbolism, because Heaven may just want to get your attention and say hello.

For your reference, on the following page is a numerology chart, which reveals the numerical vibrations of letters. I recommend researching numerologists' teachings for additional numerical meanings if you find this of interest. You can figure out the numerical vibration of anything with letters, including your name, by adding the digits associated with the letters. For instance, for my name, Mary Soliel, I add 4 + 1 + 9 + 7 for my first name and 1 + 6 + 3 + 9 + 5 + 3 for my last name. All these numbers add up to 48. I add 4 + 8 to get 12. These numbers can be added once again: 1 + 2 = 3. My full name carries the energy of the number 3. If you get to a master number, such as 11, 22, or 33, numerologists suggest that you don't reduce to a single digit.

1	2	3	4	5	6	7	8	9
A	B	C	D	E	F	G	H	I
J	K	L	M	N	O	P	Q	R
S	T	U	V	W	X	Y	Z	

CHAPTER 6

WE ARE MIRRORS FOR
EACH OTHER

*H*ave you ever seen someone for the first time, and the moment your eyes meet, you feel you know that person already? That is probably because you know him or her on a soul level, from a previous lifetime or probably multiple lifetimes. You've surely heard the phrase "Eyes are the windows to the soul." If the feeling is especially profound, this person may be one of your soul mates.

I have experienced a handful of beautiful and unforgettable reunions where the moment I've seen my closest soul connections, I've instantly lost all sense of time and space. First the person is there, perhaps twenty feet away, and then the person is here, just a few feet away, as if some frames from a movie have been cut. My acute focus is on that person, and awareness of everything else just drifts away. Synchronicity is at an all-time high, mirroring the deep connectedness. Without a doubt, I know that these people are the souls that were closest to me in previous lifetimes. When this happens, I feel somewhat nervous and excited inside as the meeting will bring up and flood my being with long-held memories, which I may eventually explore.

They aren't necessarily past lovers, although most of us think of soul mates in the romantic sense. Our soul mates also embody other types of relationships. They may have been, or are in this life, a parent, a sibling, a child, a grandparent, a close friend, or even a co-worker or colleague. We share with our soul mates deeper relationships. They consist of different kinds of relationships from life to life and we mostly stay with these same souls lifetime after lifetime. Thus, the soul who was your brother in one life may be your best friend in the next.

Undeniably, I share with both of my children deep soul connections, as we know we have journeyed through many lifetimes together. Even though we have different personalities, who we are on a soul level are very similar, and we are extremely compatible and deeply close. Having this kind of awareness only richens our present life experience.

For many years, I did not believe in reincarnation. However, I had always been curious about it, even as a child. About a decade ago, everything changed when I read *Only Love Is Real* and *Many Lives, Many Masters* by Brian L. Weiss, MD. As a successful and highly reputable psychiatrist, Dr. Weiss was skeptical of the concept of past lives. After an exhaustive yet unsuccessful effort to help one patient using conventional therapies, Dr. Weiss led her into a hypnotic trance. When he regressed her to the time when her symptoms first arose, this woman went back to a whole different lifetime. This and subsequent experiences changed Dr. Weiss's life and career. Reading his books changed mine as well.

I eventually decided to study hypnotherapy and become a hypnotherapist. As a student, I had a similar experience when hypnotizing a fellow therapist-in-training. I led my practice client into trance to explore a memory in her present life, but she eventually went deep into a violent and painful past life that sent shivers down my spine. It was a place her subconscious needed to take her in order to release the tragic memories.

Soon after graduation, I led a past-lives group regression for several of us who'd studied hypnotherapy together. We knew we were all connected and weren't surprised to find out, during the session, that each of us had known at least one other in a past life. I'll never forget when one woman saw herself and me as children, living in an orphanage. She knew me from my smile and said I was very gifted in pencil-drawing portraits. This present-day friend didn't know me well enough to know that pencil drawing is a talent of mine in this life too and that my best drawings are portraits. We do carry our talents from lifetime to lifetime.

Synchronicity often unveils significant past-life memories that need to surface and be healed. Several years ago, I had one of those loss-of-time-and-space moments when I met Maya, my immediately realized soul mate friend. Maya had lived all over the world in exotic and exciting places and yet somehow, with her husband and three children, resided for a short time in a suburb of Detroit, just a mile from where I lived.

The recollection of how the Universe brought us together, with her having trotted the globe since childhood and me having lived my whole life in the state of Michigan, still fills me with wonder. We became immediately close and knew that our connection ran deep. From the beginning, we talked almost daily, and I recall feeling the need to share so much so quickly because, on some level, I knew that our time together was limited.

One day, we met to take our young kids swimming. Maya told me how, just days before, her young son had started to go under in the water and she'd jumped into the pool with her clothes on to save him. At one point, while we chatted by the pool, my four-year-old daughter got out of the pool to go to the bathroom. When she returned, she forgot to put on her "floaties" and just went straight in. I too had to jump in and save her.

Maya kept saying she was *so* sorry she hadn't gone in herself. She apologized profusely, expressing much frustration. I told her to just let it go, that my daughter was fine now and that's all that mattered. I was just trying to recover from the scare and concentrate on knowing that all was well.

I knew that her reaction had to do with more than the fact that Maya was wearing a swimsuit and wanted to spare me getting my clothes wet, but I never really understood the meaning behind these related scenarios for years. We were both awed by the alarming, but powerful, synchronicity that we'd each saved our kids in the same way within just days of each other. There was definitely something behind this that was beyond our conscious understanding.

Six years passed before I understood the deeper meaning behind that synchronicity. While in trance, I went to a past life where I was happily married and had a beautiful little girl. One day, my husband and I took our child to a lake to swim. I asked him to watch our child while I left for a short while. Our little girl drowned; he somehow couldn't save her in time. Utterly distraught and unable to live life without my child, I committed suicide in that life. I left my great love to wallow in his own desperate grief, guilt, and despair. I immediately recognized the man in this past life as Maya in this life—just one of our many lifetimes together.

I recalled with shock and amazement the original synchronicities involving Maya and our kids that had brought up this tragic past-life experience that desperately needed healing. That's when I learned without a doubt that synchronicity will unveil that which needs to be healed from the past. You can imagine the karma this brought up in this lifetime, a very deep bond filled with beautiful yet painful moments. I dreadfully abandoned her in that lifetime, and she abandoned me in this one—albeit in a different way, most thankfully—but a karmic debt was painfully paid with overwhelming grief.

Of course, not all soul mate reunions end sadly or tragically. On the contrary, many bring the greatest joys and can last a lifetime, especially when karmic debts have been paid or at least cleared, both people are at the same level of understanding, and the connections are destined to be pursued. Soul mate relationships always invite the best opportunities for spiritual growth. When you find these souls, you may feel a sense of ecstasy, for you are experiencing a cosmic reunion of sorts. You read each other's thoughts and finish each other's sentences—not just years, months, or even weeks after meeting, but right away. You marvel at the wondrous synchronicities you witness together.

You feel as if you and your soul mates are best friends immediately, before you've even gotten to know them in this life. You might not like the same foods, clothes, or cars, but on a deeper, soul level, it's as if you are cut from the same cloth. That is why these connections are your greatest mirrors. We are all mirrors for each other: people you meet on the street, at the supermarket, and so on. But you see yourself best, the very core of who you are, when you are in the company of your soul mates, as well as other members of your "soul family." Those in your soul family also stay with you lifetime after lifetime, but they aren't as strongly bonded to you as your soul mates.

By the way, for those of you looking for your soul mate of the romantic type, you need to allow the Universe to provide opportunities for the two of you to meet. Listen to your gut feelings. Of course, the time has to be right, and you both need to be ready. If you feel compelled to take that community class or sign up for that group hike, just do it. Your future partner may be getting the same "vibes" too. Destiny will make sure you meet, but what happens next is up to each of you, because free will reigns. Of course, with the exception of online dating, it's hard to meet people when you are holed up at home, unless that gorgeous hunk of a carpet cleaner knocks on your door.

Anyone can unwittingly act as our mirror, often in the most unexpected ways. One day, I was driving along, minding my own business, and a man in the car next to me flipped me off. I truly did not know what had caused him to do that, and it was very unsettling. I arrived at the grocery store, and the clerk was obviously in a very angry mood and took it out on me.

Later that day, I spoke with a stranger on the phone who was trying to sell me something, and she was unkind, as well. I couldn't understand why people were treating me so awfully on this particular day. Then I realized I needed to just stop, think, and ask what they could be mirroring to me. Author Shakti Gawain first taught me through her transformative book, *Living in the Light*, that the world is our mirror. Suddenly, it became clear. Indeed, I was angry with myself! Yes, they mirrored what I needed to heal within, and I had drawn them into my life on this day. Oh, thank you, people, for the finger and the angry words. I got the message.

A similar situation happened just this morning when I woke with worry. I thought I'd cleared myself of the negative thoughts, but I still felt some fear, specifically about money issues. After dropping off the kids at school, three different cars at different times nearly hit me—three close calls within a very short time frame. One woman who was at a stop sign when I had the right of way didn't even look for oncoming traffic as she started to pull in front of me. To top it off, she gave me a dirty look and waved her arms around as if it were my fault.

After the third incident, I firmly got hold of the fact that I was creating this and needed to let go of the negativity and worry regarding money issues. I knew better than this. I released my anger at others for their reckless driving and continued on with my day in a much better mood.

I know that when I go out on the road from now on, I'll be driving among good, aware, and peaceful drivers, because I shifted my energy and like attracts like. Just like a magnet, instead of attracting the panicky, stressful, and angry drivers (which reflected my panicky, stressful, and angry thoughts this morning), I'll attract the opposite. If this all sounds like nonsense, explore what your thoughts are compared to your reality at any given time. Keep in mind that the time it takes for our thoughts to manifest is lessening dramatically as we continue to evolve. Sometimes our thoughts manifest into an immediate experience, such as when I hit the skunk.

In addition to our thoughts, our behaviors and actions are also creating our experiences. When someone keeps attracting a mate or friend with a common negative quality, such as a tendency to be manipulative, that should not be seen as a punishment by any means. Perhaps this person hasn't learned to set boundaries in relationships. Therefore, she will attract people who manipulate her in various ways. If she allows herself to be controlled, a master manipulator may be on the horizon. When our relationships aren't working, instead of holding onto our anger or frustration, we need to ask ourselves what is being mirrored to us. Then we can bless, rather than detest, the suffering endured and change what needs to be changed, once and for all.

Let me make it clear that synchronicity does not always make our lives easier. It often pushes us toward spiritual growth, and that is usually challenging. We attract just the people we need to, through synchronicity and destiny, sometimes with karmic ties, in order to mirror something so that, ultimately, we grow. As we become more enlightened, we bless *all* meetings that the Universe sets up.

When things go wrong or we feel overwhelmed with difficulties, the phrase "This too shall pass" can be a very powerful affirmation to think or speak in the moment and can help us stop focusing on the negative aspects of what is occurring. These four words—and the feeling behind the words—have gotten me through some difficult times, because the hard times always do pass. Because change is constant, there are always new opportunities, potentials, healings, and experiences on the horizon. It's hard to see this during those most troubling moments, but when you say these four words, the situation doesn't feel as burdensome. Additionally, speaking or thinking these words demonstrates your intention that the problem will be only a temporary setback or challenge, because focusing on it can cause the situation to linger.

Have you noticed that when you're feeling extra good about yourself—extra proud, extra happy, or extra relaxed—you often attract people of a similar state? And have you noticed that when you feel the opposite emotions, you attract people that are reflecting that as well? When I'm feeling down about something, I breathe deeply and remind myself that the feelings are just temporary, and although they need to be honored, they can change on a dime.

I think we often hold the misbelief that it takes something or someone else to get us out of our funk. After we process our feelings and determine that it's time to let go of our negativity, we can take charge of our mood. One of my favorite things to tell clients is, "Fake it till you make it!" Fake your joy, happiness, wealth, and all you desire until you actually create it. This is a fun and easy way to tap into the magnificent power of your imagination. We can share this practice with others, and it can become contagious.

Next time you're having dinner with your significant other, have a conversation in which you make believe you've just received a windfall and you can use the money to take your dream cruise on the Mediterranean, for example. Become mirrors for each other, and mimic the excitement for what you desire—in wonderful detail. Have fun with your imaginations.

A less proactive way in which we act as mirrors is when we are channeling messages for others, usually without knowing it. Have you ever sat across from a friend who needed help with a problem or concern, and you suddenly found that words started coming out of your mouth that you weren't really thinking of, words that wouldn't have normally come out of you? And that person had a "light bulb moment" or heard just what he or she needed to move forward? That may be because your angels were using you as a tool for getting a message or guidance across to the one who needed to hear it.

This often happens to me, on both giving and receiving ends. If I'm the giver of information, it helps to tap into my intuition as these messages will flow easily. As a receiver of information, friends will say something unexpected to me, and after the initial surprise, they will tell me that they don't know why they said it. I consider this Divine intervention and always a blessing, even when the message is difficult to swallow.

Before I met my husband, I knew a man whom I thought I would eventually marry. He lived out of state, and just days prior to visiting him, while getting an allergy shot, the nurse accidentally gave me too much serum. I literally went white and had what was later determined to be a panic attack as a result of the shock to my system. This started a chain of panic attacks over a period of time. Anything emotional, either good or bad, could set off some very frightening, though not dangerous, symptoms.

As a result, I maintained distance from anything that could set me off emotionally, including this wonderful man. I was too embarrassed to tell him what was going on. The thought of having a panic attack in front of him was scary, and I felt he would misunderstand the source. Misunderstandings ensued anyway, and it was the beginning of the end of our relationship, at least from my perspective.

I was talking to my friend Julie about it some time later and told her that I had really messed things up. She said that I wouldn't have been able to have children with him had we married. Then she said she didn't know why she'd spoken those words; they'd just come out. I knew she channeled that, and I accepted that as truth. I needed to have my two precious children, and I needed to know that this man, a definite soul connection, existed. However, we weren't destined to be together in this lifetime. I believe that the overloaded allergy shot and the panic attacks were all part of the plan.

So when someone, a friend or even a stranger, tells you something and then says, "I don't know why I just said that," or "I wasn't thinking that—it just came out," there may be a Divine message for you that can give you peace, understanding, direction, perspective, or a dose of reality. Allow the mirror to reflect the wisdom.

CHAPTER 7

GLIMPSES OF THE FUTURE

Synchronicity provides clues to upcoming events in your life and in the world. These signs are to be blessed, whether you deem the events good or bad because they help you prepare for the future. Knowing the Universe is giving you a preview feels like you are being wrapped up in a warm blanket with the security of never being alone. The coming attraction may cause you to anticipate joy. Or sometimes, it prepares you for a potential blow. In any case, it allows you to rise above the situation and see things from a higher perspective.

When my family lived in New Mexico, we sometimes had scorpions and centipedes in our house. If I saw either type of these uninvited guests, I would consider it as a symbol of a "sting" or that of being "stung." However, I hadn't seen either creature in the two years we lived in Colorado. Yet one day, right in the middle of our family room, I saw a centipede. I immediately knew that it was warning me. Not only was I sure I was going to get stung by someone, but I also intuited who would sting me. Sure enough, the very next day, I learned that this person did, indeed, do an upsetting thing behind my back. But feeling the support of the Universe, I could view things from a higher place and thus I coped much better having been given this heads up.

There have been a few memorable times when I've stepped in gum and then shortly afterward found myself in a very "sticky" situation. Someone's careless and thoughtless action of leaving their gum on the ground ended up forewarning me of the situation ahead. Therefore, I handled the situation better.

By far the most difficult signs I've ever encountered occurred throughout most of 2001, when I had 911 synchronicities. I saw those three numbers repeatedly, sometimes one time right after another and often in association with seeing or hearing sirens from emergency vehicles. For instance, when my kids and I were at a water park, I went to purchase food at a booth. The total bill was $9.11. Just as I was told the amount due, an ambulance drove right past me on a wide sidewalk. It was an unexpected place to see any type of vehicle. I felt that the repetitive signs, over a period of several months, were warning me that some kind of emergency was going to occur in my personal life. I eventually became convinced that something awful was going to happen, specifically on September 11 of that year, and that I needed to be prepared for it.

The day before September 11, my friend Lisa and I went for a long hike in open space near the Sandia Mountains. At one point, we decided—or perhaps were guided to without realizing it—to call for the hawks. We summoned the magnificent birds, literally called out for their presence. Lisa really loves hawks, as do I. They are wonderfully significant messengers. We couldn't see any in the sky at the time. Suddenly and from what seemed out of nowhere, four hawks came and circled above us.

We were overwhelmed by the power and synchronicity of it all. Neither of us had ever seen four hawks flying together. Usually, you see them flying by themselves. It truly was a miracle. We kept watching the hawks, not wanting the spectacular sight to end. At one point, one of them left the group of four and flew off. At the time, we just celebrated the most remarkable display of nature. However, the next day we realized that the hawks were showing us a glimpse of the future—a most tragic glimpse.

On the morning of 9/11, I woke up feeling very dizzy. Without having gotten out of bed or even having moved my head yet, the room was already spinning. I eventually got up and went to my husband, who was aware of my concern about all the 911 synchronicity I was experiencing, and I told him, "It's 9/11 today, so prepare." Just then, he turned on the

TV, and there we saw the World Trade Center after the first plane hit the North Tower.

The realization hit me that the four hawks that Lisa and I saw the day before represented the four places of impact on September 11. The fourth one (which flew away) represented the changed course of Flight 93, as I saw it. I know that many felt the events of 9/11 coming in different ways. No one may have known the specifics of what was going to happen, but on a deep level, many people knew that a terrible tragedy was about to occur.

Synchronicity can also clue us in on our most significant, personal life events. A week before Jack proposed to me, we went to a restaurant that served excellent Chinese food. I saw that the fortune inside my cookie read, "You will soon marry." We had not once spoken of marriage at that point. I didn't tell him what my fortune read, and, strangely, he didn't ask. Yet one week later, he proposed. I've opened hundreds of fortune cookies over the years, and never before or since have I received a fortune regarding marriage.

There were signs from the beginning that our marriage would not last "forever." When planning the wedding ceremony, my priest asked us to choose one of two Bible passages for him to read. I liked one, but I wanted it to end a verse early because the word *divorce* was mentioned, and I didn't want that word in our ceremony. The priest agreed. However, to my dismay and shock, during the actual ceremony, the priest not only kept it in but also mentioned in his sermon that I wanted the word in there because I didn't fear it; he fully misconstrued my direct request. From a higher perspective, that was the first sign.

When choosing our wedding song, I asked the band to play "You and I" by Stevie Wonder; it was later sung by my favorite talent, Barbra Streisand. At one point, the song talks about finding somebody "that may not be here forever to see me through." This bothered me, but I loved the song so much, and Jack agreed to it. When I checked with my friends for their opinion, they said that a lot of wedding songs say something dramatic and that if I really liked it, I should go ahead with it, so I did.

One night, nearly sixteen years later, I asked Jack for a divorce. We both knew our marriage wasn't working, and there was no blame either way, but I couldn't continue on that path any longer. We were both deeply upset, and in the wee hours of the next morning, I went for a drive just to be alone. I was thinking about these very synchronicities that mirrored the future reality of our marriage ending. Just then, I noticed that the personalized license plate on the truck in front of me read "YOU N I," the title of our wedding song. I cried with extreme gratitude for this validation from the Universe. I wanted to thank whoever was driving that truck so late that night, who unknowingly gave me the comfort I desperately needed.

Soon after I made the decision that it was time to ask Jack for a divorce, I was at a conference and found myself sitting next to a woman who had an unusual last name. When I asked her about it, she told me it wasn't her true name; rather she'd given it to herself when she divorced. She then referred to something she'd written in her notes. It said, "When I put myself first, everyone wins." Of course, I hadn't told this person what had been going through my mind just prior to meeting her. Little did I know, I too would have a new last name. And that quotation became my strength in future months and years. What would seem an uneventful meeting held tremendous meaning for me.

And speaking of partings, just before my soul mate friend, Maya, and I became estranged, I was listening to the radio in my home. As soon as a particular song came on, my five-year-old daughter said, "Listen, Mom. It's yours and Maya's favorite song!" The name of the song was "Don't Speak," and in it, the band No Doubt sings about two friends spending much time together and one friend realizing, "I'm losing my best friend."

True, we did spend a lot of time together, several get-togethers a week, but she had recently moved to the Pacific Northwest. Now, this was not a song I ever talked about. It wasn't a song that Maya mentioned either, so I thought it strange for my daughter to say it was our favorite song. However, a few months before, it was synchronistically the very song that was playing on the radio just as I drove up to her family's home when their moving van had arrived. I thought the song was mirroring the fact that she was moving and that I was losing my friend in that way.

My daughter seemed to channel this so that I would be prepared for something much more upsetting. Soon after that preview of my future, there was a meltdown between Maya and me, and our friendship abruptly ended. I was devastated but prepared for it.

Years probably passed before a day would go by without thinking of my soul mate friend. Imagine not fitting in with most others: you're different, you think differently, and you care about different things. No one *really* understands you. And in a single moment, everything changes, and you meet someone who is your mirror. You don't feel alone, and when you're with that person, you see the best of who you really are. We had lifetimes of knowledge and understanding of each other. That is, until I lost my mirror. Eventually, I learned that I didn't need the mirror to know who I was. Yet, I saw it as a blessed gift that reflected what I already knew.

Once, when taking a road trip to Sedona, Arizona, with my family, "Don't Speak" came on the radio. After a few bars, it stopped playing and then restarted. Then after several more bars, it did the same, and kept returning to the beginning of the song. We were amazed. It happened at least ten times, and we couldn't understand how the station couldn't have corrected the technical problem quicker. I'd never heard such a repetitive error on the radio before. All four of us were laughing, but for me, it was about much more than a radio station's technical problems.

It seemed as if the error with the song had happened just for me, because it perfectly reflected the sadness I kept reliving over and over again—the sadness was a "broken record." On an even deeper and more significant level, it was a broken record of grief over many lifetimes. This strange occurrence could have happened with any song, but it had happened with this very song. This was an astounding synchronicity that is a perfect example of the mirrors that occur in our lives, not just with people and with songs, but with anything ... even trains.

When living in Michigan, Maya and I took a short two-day Amtrak train trip to Chicago. We had a fabulously fun time, filled with unforgettable synchronicities, which was par for the course whenever we were together. When we got caught in a rainstorm on a cold afternoon, the only place we found close by for shelter was a coffee shop. It just happened to have a huge fireplace, where we could dry our drenched jackets, have a nice long talk while drinking coffee, and wait out the rain—perfect. We always felt "watched over."

On the trip back home on the train, I don't know what was in the air, but Maya told me a funny story, and that got us started on this kick of uncontrollable laughter that lasted most of the trip home. I never laughed so much or so hard about nothing in all my life. You know you're with a soul connection when you can just lose it with uncontrollable laughter for no reason.

Perhaps you're laughing about lifetimes of things that happened between you without even realizing it.

Several years later when in New Mexico, I heard a commercial on the radio, and to the best of my recollection, it said something like this: "Wouldn't it be great to take a train ride with your best friend and have uncontrollable laughter? Ride Amtrak from Albuquerque to Chicago." It was utterly surreal. The description of uncontrollable laughter with a best friend on an Amtrak train was synchronistic enough, but "from Albuquerque to *Chicago*"? How extraordinary was that? I wondered how many people take the train all the way from Albuquerque to Chicago and couldn't understand why Amtrak would market their business in that way. My family and I once took the train from Albuquerque to Los Angeles; it would have made more marketing sense to target the destination of LA to New Mexicans, in my opinion.

This was Divine intervention at its peak, and I heard that commercial several times. It validated the importance of our connection in this life, and it most definitely kept it alive. When relationships cease in person, I believe they continue on in spirit, certainly our closest connections. I share these synchronicities I experienced regarding Maya to convey how synchronicity will mirror your most significant soul connections in a multitude of ways, and will move you toward the necessary healings and a deeper recognition of your most important relationships.

Sometimes the synchronicities we experience don't appear to give deeply meaningful glimpses of the future; they are simple and seemingly insignificant. For instance, on this morning, as I walked toward the coffee shop to start writing, I became particularly aware of cracks in the bricks of buildings in this quaint downtown near where I live. I didn't know why I suddenly noticed this for the first time, but I just did. Later this day, I watched a movie, and at one point, this man picked at a crack in the outside wall with a stick, saying to his wife, "Oh, look. It's a new crack." It's as if present and future are blending together.

On a recent Sunday afternoon, while eating lunch in a restaurant, two determined flies kept attacking my food. I shooed them away repeatedly. My meal became more about them than about the food. I'd never seen such persistent flies, and I felt there was something more to it but did not know what it was. When I returned home, I popped in a movie from my DVD library, *The Bridges of Madison County*. It had caught my eye that morning when I was straightening out my closet; I decided I would watch it later in the day.

To my amazement, I watched Meryl Streep's character shoo flies away—flies all over the food, flies all over the place—throughout that whole movie. Not only did I appreciate director Clint Eastwood's realistic portrayal of farm life in Iowa, with his considerable attention to detail, I realized that I was destined to watch this movie. Did it mean that I would one day meet my own "Robert Kincaid," may suddenly feel the urge to take up photography, or desire to go to Iowa to see the covered bridges? I still don't really know, but I hope it is the former. Or, perhaps it was just a good movie for me to see at the time, for some reason. But the synchronicity was undeniable.

When your reality unveils a confirmation of the previous experienced event as described above, no matter how simple or complex, it is so comforting. You feel that you are exactly where you need to be and doing what you need to be doing for whatever reason, even though it is oftentimes unknown.

My glimpses of the future have increased significantly with the writing of this book. I'm at the point now that I hear or see from people, the radio or television, signage, billboards, or situations things that immediately mirror my own prior words, thoughts, or experiences. I wonder if part of our evolution is that we'll become increasingly telepathic, and our communication won't always need to be voiced. Additionally, we'll more easily adapt to situations and challenges as we get glimpses before they occur.

What glimpses are you receiving about your own life? How comfortable are you with getting previews? If you, deep down, don't want to know what's ahead or fear the future, you may be closing the window to awareness.

CHAPTER 8

SIGNS UNCOVER POTENTIALS

I believe that we choose our life circumstances prior to incarnating. Our parents, siblings, geographic location, and all other basic elements of our lives are already determined on a soul level in inter-life, the life between lives, to create the optimal conditions for our souls' growth. We come into the perfect setup to achieve the desired movement on our spiritual journey.

We also predetermine the general framework for our adult lives: whom we marry, what we do, and the people we meet along the way. You may have heard that we actually create spiritual contracts. Synchronicity illuminates all these predetermined aspects of our lives. Yet because we have free will, we can "rewrite" the contracts. Sometimes things change, certainly when subject to the free will of others, and we need to reset the course. For instance, if a predestined mate chooses someone else, then one needs to consider plan B. We are always free to choose. My personal choice has always been to follow my destined path, to surrender to it.

Our given names can sometimes reflect our destined paths. For instance, is it merely coincidence that arguably the world's greatest golfer is named Tiger *Woods?* Is it purely by chance that the mother of Buzz Aldrin, the second man to step foot on the moon, had the maiden name *Moon*? How about the dermatologist named Dr. *Boyle*? Or Dr. *Payne*, the dentist? I believe all these people followed their destined professions. Of course, our destinies are about more than our careers—they are also, and probably more importantly, about our relationships.

Author Paulo Coelho so beautifully writes in his novel *Eleven Minutes*, "I realize that I didn't go into that café by chance; really important meetings are planned by the souls long before the bodies see each other." Oh yes, our souls do plan these meetings, and that's why we feel that déjà vu when we meet those with whom we have sacred contracts. These events were planned ahead of time. The meetings are so rich, so intense, even when you're not consciously aware of the significance. But when you are aware, the feelings are especially grand.

The signs of destiny were present when I met Jack, my future husband. We met at a computer exposition—not the most romantic setting—where we were working at each of our company's booths. When walking up to where he stood, I saw a few people lining up to speak with him. Before we uttered a word to each other, I saw him from several feet away and immediately thought, "I'm going to marry you and have children with you." It was an inner perception, not love at first sight but a profound knowingness at first sight, which I had never felt before. I "knew him," but I didn't know him yet. He was very handsome, with twinkling eyes, rosy cheeks, and a nice and well-maintained beard and mustache.

I felt a connection with him that was deeper than mere physical attraction, even though I have always gone weak around guys with beards. It wasn't until years into our marriage that I realized we'd shared past lives. When we met, I wasn't consciously aware of this because the concept of past lives was not a part of my belief system.

In hindsight, I can say that synchronicity brought me to his booth. Earlier this day, when on my way to begin working my own booth, I "happened" to walk by this man's co-worker, a guy I had known in college. We hadn't seen each other in years. He invited me to a gathering of his colleagues that evening, and of course Jack was there. Destiny made sure of that.

I firmly believe we "contracted" in inter-life for the union of marriage. That's why I had that feeling of "knowingness at first sight." I also believe we "contracted" for divorce as well. This may sound far-fetched, and I say this not because I've invented a way to feel better about my decisions, especially about putting my children through the emotional upheaval. I always want the truth and take responsibility for it. However, my firm belief is that our relationship was predestined, all of it. The purpose of our coming together was to have our two children, learn from each other, and then have the courage to go our separate ways for the growth of all our souls. Yes, I believe that my children, too, when their souls chose us to be their parents, knew of the strong potential for divorce as well.

Some people are blessed with a happy marriage that lasts a lifetime, and it's a beautiful thing. Others are blessed with several relationships that bring them impressive soul growth, and that can be beautiful, too, despite the hardships and challenges. Many people I personally know had unhappy first relationships, but those relationships caused them to heal what they needed to heal. Their soul mates were then attracted to them, because they were prepared for it. Those unhappy relationships that they had the courage to release were blessings!

My parents have one of those marriages that last forever. Observing them as a married couple over the years has been like watching two people dance a beautiful waltz—flowing with sure step, independent as two separate beings, and yet in sync, one complementing the other, classy, engaging, an effortless meld.

Our most significant relationships—whether family members, romantic partnerships, close friendships, or even professional relationships—are often with those we have been with in many lifetimes. They are closest to us, in the way of the heart. Also, we travel in soul groups and find ourselves pulled toward places where we can meet our soul family.

In recent years, I've often heard people say that they moved somewhere not because of any specific reason, such as a job opportunity, but because they felt pulled to this new geographic location by an inner feeling. Additionally, I've had friends and acquaintances who moved away from New Mexico, for instance, but felt pulled back, and I believe it was because they left their soul family as well as a land they felt connected to.

My friend, Clare, left New Mexico for an eighteen-month journey through the eastern and midwestern United States in search of her next location to live, only to find herself back in the "Land of Enchantment," continuing to live her passion as a sculptor. Another woman I know of, from Santa Fe, moved all the way to the East Coast and then, after only one day, decided to move back. Soon after she did, she met her soul mate and they married. We are congregating with our soul families in order to connect with like-minded people, living in geographic areas that suit us on deeper levels, as we move toward positive change in this world.

We can also be pulled toward places for unexpected reasons. I learned from *The Light Shall Set You Free*, that New Mexico holds the karma for the creation of the atomic bomb. Yes, not only people but also places, cities, states, and countries acquire karma, which manifest though the Law of Cause and Effect. Karma says that for every action, there is a reaction. People, without knowing why, have been driven to settle in this region to balance the karma and provide accelerated healing energy to this area. I read this just after feeling the pull myself, a perfectly timed sign, one of the countless New Mexico signs that proved to be validating.

Synchronicity stepped in again with a great force when it was time to follow the destiny of this move to New Mexico. But it happened in a very roundabout way and over quite some time. I remember watching a television show about a place in Arizona that had amazing red rocks, which attracted metaphysical and spiritual seekers. I couldn't recall the name of the city, though.

One morning shortly thereafter, I woke with a strong message that it was in my family's highest interest that we move to another state. I held a small laminated map in my hands and instantly knew that the state was Arizona. That day, my mother and I were in the car waiting at a red light, and a truck made a turn into the oncoming lane next to us. It made that turn very slowly, and we had a full, lingering side view of that truck.

In huge letters was the word *AriZona*. I mean, it moved *so* slow and was such a large truck that I couldn't help but smile, saying in my mind, "Okay, Universe, I get it!" I don't recall ever seeing an AriZona Tea truck before or since that sighting, and it happened to appear on the day I had been given a message that would eventually change the direction of our lives.

Weeks later, my parents, who were unaware that I was pondering our family's move to the Southwest (no one knew at the time), told me they were planning, for the first time, to spend the winter in Arizona. Synchronicity seemed to be lining everything up. Visiting them would be a perfect way to scope out the area, and—who knows?—maybe they'd move there too if they really liked it. This seemed to be working out amazingly well. I later learned that the name of that place in Arizona that had the beautiful red rocks was Sedona.

During that trip to see my parents, I saw and immediately fell in love with Sedona. That first view of the red rocks took my breath away—I felt like I was on another planet. With such young children, I wasn't traveling much in those days, that is, until I found Sedona. I was somehow able to visit there three times in that one year. But this was a tourist destination with a very high cost of living.

Moving to Sedona seemed highly unrealistic. How would my husband make a living there? What saddened me was how much city life was encroaching on the natural environment, but I still found it irresistible and truly mesmerizing, and I sought out more isolated places to hike in. As my love for the desert landscape and connection to this part of the earth grew strong, I asked God to show me an "affordable Sedona."

The next phase of the revelations came on a day when I met someone who soon became a close friend, and we somehow both uttered on that first meeting how we wished we lived in the Southwest. Nearly a year later, she asked me to go with her on a trip to New Mexico to help her scope out a place to live. I had been intrigued by New Mexico for many years, in a mysterious sort of way. Perhaps on some level I knew we were destined to live there. I was about to receive the answer to my prayer and God would show me my "affordable Sedona" through my friend on this trip.

My whole being resonated with New Mexico, from the moment we arrived. As we searched for a place for her to live, we drove toward the village where I intuitively knew my family would actually end up residing. Everything became crystal clear.

Over several months, all the details fell into place, and we prepared for our move. When it came time to look for a house for my family, I was able to find and put an offer on a fabulous southwestern stucco home in just a single weekend. Everything came so easily once we decided to move, and that ease further validated that we were on the right path. To top it off, just prior to returning to Michigan after my successful house-hunting trip, I felt so "lucky" that I went into the local casino and hit a $1,000 jackpot on a slot machine. But the fact is, we really hit the jackpot in a much more important and blessed way.

There was a significant reason for us to move to New Mexico. I trusted that my son, who was on constant asthma medications in Michigan, would fare better in the high desert mountain climate. Destiny and my guidance were driving us to move and health was the driving reason.

I recalled when, prior to even considering a move, I'd asked Scott's allergist if he would be better off in a different area of the country (without mentioning a particular state). He said that you never know, but if you have the choice between, say, a humid climate or the mountains of New Mexico, you should choose New Mexico. He emphasized that there was no guarantee and that it depends on the person. So that was a synchronistic clue.

Sure enough, Scott was soon off daily medications after our move, following the unexpected healing by the pastor (as described in the chapter "Nature Speaks"). I know that the more conducive climate played a part in his improved health, as well. Although, I cannot prove what ultimately caused the dramatic shift in his condition, the bottom line is that synchronicity called for us to bravely leave family and friends and move to where we were guided, and I surrendered to that guidance. Even though health reasons were the main impetus for our move, things often happen for a multitude of reasons. And it was an unfolding, a never-ending unfolding, as the miracles of Divine guidance continued.

After five years of living in New Mexico, we needed to move to Colorado. A month after the divorce, we settled in a town near Boulder. Following the move, I recalled the time back when we lived in Michigan when I'd told Jack of my prediction that we would live in Colorado in ten years. Ten years later, we *did* find ourselves in Colorado, with an unknown detour to New Mexico, divorced and in two separate homes, but all of us were in Colorado a decade down the road. It was all predestined. Until these moves, I lived my whole life in Michigan, and Jack lived most of his adult life there, so the thought of the four of us moving away from family and friends seemed hardly predictable at the time.

I was deeply saddened when we left New Mexico. My kids and Jack, too, felt pulled away from a place that we were connected to, what felt like our true home. Even though I have always embraced change, this was one change I found very difficult. I am a desert girl, through and through. I felt a deep tie to this land. The way light touches the earth there, the huge sky, and the stunning cloud formations—all emanate unique and mysterious beauty, like nowhere else I know. It's a feeling difficult to articulate, and it took hold of me and did not want to let go. However, this move, validated by a new chain of synchronicities, was right for my family. And I held strong to that knowledge.

Synchronicity helped me to see and adjust to the bigger picture. I was driving through Boulder with my friend Karen and told her that even though Colorado was extremely beautiful and I felt that we needed to be here, I was having a hard time living away from New Mexico. Just as I spoke those words, we saw a large box turtle right in front of us, on a residential street, no less. My friend said that in the more than a dozen years that she'd lived in the Boulder area, she had never seen a turtle anywhere in town.

Karen asked, "You know what a turtle means, don't you?" She had previously nicknamed me the "goddess of synchronicity," knowing just how much I respect and follow signs. "It means you carry your home wherever you go," she informed me. Oh, thank you, friend, as well as the turtle that suddenly appeared at the perfect moment, for being my messengers.

Despite the challenges, I've learned to trust and let go. Good things come out of all difficulties and change. Because we are constantly presented with change, we need to embrace it more than ever, in these transformational times of the new millennium. We continuously get opportunities to practice our acceptance of it.

Following Divine guidance, your gut instincts, and the magic of synchronicity can be simple at times and challenging at other times. They'll guide you to the people you need to be with. They present your unfolding destiny. They may move you toward tremendous change. Of course, you always have free will to make your own choices. If you stay true to what is in your highest interests, the gift of awareness will reveal itself in miraculous and unimaginable ways that will support your growth and destiny.

CHAPTER 9

EXPECT THE UNEXPECTED

*H*ow I've always loved this phrase. To expect the unexpected is a powerful declaration that you are fully open to the unfolding, that you are ready for miracles, and that you are counting on possibilities that will often awe and amaze. The unexpected can change your life for the better in ways you never dreamed. Let your life unfold without pushing so hard. Set goals and take the necessary actions, but don't be rigid in your ideas of how you're going to get from point A to point B. This will invite the Divine to grace you.

Since I was a little girl, I placed expectations on everything. I expected certain reactions from my family, friends, and authority figures. I prematurely decided how most everything would play out in my life, like scenes in a play. I constantly set myself up for disappointment when reality deviated from my strong desires. Things rarely turned out the way they played out in my mind.

As a mature adult, in my mid-thirties actually, I finally saw the light. It became a very freeing practice to reduce mental chatter and emotional energy by just letting things happen instead of holding unrealistic expectations that would eventually be doomed. The phrase "Let go and let God" carried significant meaning for me.

Much of this book has been channeled. For the most part, I cannot easily distinguish, beyond the recounting of my memories, between my own thoughts and what I'm being helped and guided with. I'm always being whispered to. I believe we all are, especially when we open up to our higher selves, the angels, Divine guidance, and most certainly through synchronicity. We may not hear an actual sound or voice; silent impressions of knowingness in our minds may signal us to turn right instead of left, prompt us to recall revealing words to a song when we wake in the morning, or nudge us to look at a clock at just the right time.

The writing of this chapter feels different from the writing of the rest of this book. I feel sure that it was not at all my idea to write it, and yet I am pushed to continue.

While sitting here in the coffee shop, I asked for angelic help, because I'm not sure where to go with this chapter. The song "Good Riddance (Time of Your Life)" by Green Day came on with the words, "It's something unpredictable ... "

Yes, life is unpredictable. Things often happen in ways we never thought of, and, in the end, we ponder the events with amazement at how things actually transpired. I recall that happening when I sought to learn additional healing modalities after becoming a hypnotherapist.

When I studied hypnotherapy, I knew it was a stepping-stone to other healing work. It gave me a wonderful foundation of understanding of the mysterious and complex subconscious mind. Most importantly, I learned that we need to release from our childhood and past lives those misbeliefs that set up our adult challenges, while realizing that we do, indeed, create our realities. Hypnosis is a beautiful and natural state of mind.

Eventually, I became interested in energy work. When a practitioner worked on me energetically, it would feel so natural and miraculous. The powerful results were instantaneous; I was especially attracted to its immediacy and ease. I wanted to learn more about the mysterious workings of energy healing, balancing, and strengthening.

A couple of years after becoming a certified hypnotherapist, I visited my friend Karen, who'd just learned about an energy healing method. She demonstrated how it worked, and it immediately resonated with me. I googled it as soon as I got home, and that's when the unexpected occurred.

Not only was there a workshop teaching this method beginning the very next day somewhere in the world, but it was being held just ten minutes from my home. Obviously, it was destined that I attend, and I signed up right away. It ended up propelling me onto a whole new level in my work and personal life, which eventually resulted in the discovery of my own personal style of intuitive energetic healing.

Had I met with Karen even the following day, I would not have been able to attend the workshop until several months later. The setup was perfect. The Universal forces were in action, guiding me through each step. Nothing is more affirming than when synchronicity shows the way. And when it occurs just in the nick of time, as it so often does, this proves especially powerful. Expecting the unexpected is surrendering to synchronicity, expecting the illumination of your path in whatever way, recognizing the sign, and then being ready and willing to act.

When I began practicing healing work, I became aware of my many past lives as a healer and realized why I held a strong and natural desire to serve others in this way. Therefore, I attracted the right people in my life, people who would mirror my past and my inherent abilities. If one acts more like a free-flowing willow than a stiff oak tree—open, receptive, and moving with the pulses of life's unfolding—one can connect easily and effortlessly to the signs that guide us.

Just minutes ago, someone in the café I'm writing in asked a woman what her name was, and she loudly said, "Willow." This occurrence gave me the idea to make the point that it behooves us to act like willows rather than oaks.

Prior to my journey on my spiritual path, I thought and acted like an oak. I held fast to my beliefs. I had very strong opinions about marriage, for example; I believed that one should stay married unless something was terribly wrong. With such strict views, I would never have ventured to even consider the possibility of divorce. I mentioned earlier that there were signs, even though I tuned them out, that our marriage wouldn't last. However, there was even one more glimpse of the destined future of my marriage that occurred, and this one could not have been more unexpected.

Just before marrying Jack, I received a letter in the mail. It was sent anonymously to me, with no return address and nothing handwritten—

just a typed message. At the top of the page were the words *On His Plan For You*. It explained that I must wait for a perfect human love relationship. It said that only when I totally gave myself to Him, when I have a personal relationship with Him and loved by Him alone, would He present the perfect reflection of that relationship, in human form. It spoke of surrender, a new concept for me at that time. Who would have sent this, I wondered, and just when I was about to start a whole new life with someone? The letter greatly shocked and confused me. I ignored its message, set it aside, and would not understand its true meaning for many years.

In hindsight, I fully regard this as a preview of how my life would unfold, at least thus far—that I would begin my spiritual path and that path would come first in my life. I believe that Jack and I were destined to have our children and that we had lessons to learn for our growth. We were also destined to eventually let go of the marriage. This was not to be considered a failure, but rather a gift that allowed us to move forward on each of our soul's path. To this day, I don't know who sent me that letter almost twenty years ago, but I am convinced there was intervention from the Heavenly realms.

It is Divine grace and intervention that delivers the most blessed messages and in the most unexpected ways. My family experienced it when seeking help for my daughter, who was experiencing chronic stomachaches. We eventually found the cause of her suffering: food allergies. Karen was allergic to many common foods including dairy, tomatoes, chocolate, and peanuts. A difficult yearlong "elimination diet" was introduced by her doctor as the best solution. This would be followed by a slow reintroduction of problem foods with no promise that she would regain the normal ability to eat all the foods she desired.

When Karen's frustration with the strict diet intensified, I prayed on it, asking for guidance and help. Shortly thereafter, someone told me about NAET (Nambudripad's Allergy Elimination Techniques), a natural, noninvasive method that can eliminate allergies (for more information, go to www.naet.com). People can be cleared of allergies? I'd never heard of this as a possibility. I myself had taken several rounds of allergy shots from childhood through part of my adulthood and thought that once you were allergic to something, you basically had to live with being allergic, unless you receive allergy shots that build immunity to the allergen over a period of years. This acquaintance gave me the contact information of a naturo-path who practiced NAET.

Karen was placed on a three-month waiting list for her first appoint-ment, and it could not come soon enough. She suffered daily while doing her best to avoid those foods that we knew didn't agree with her. During this time, my friend Clare suggested that I attend a meeting with her about a new food product that helps those who suffer from food allergies. It was being held for potential investors in this newly formed company. Even though I was open to learning about the investment opportunity, I prima-rily went to find out if this health food could help my daughter. As it turned out, Clare's invitation proved to be a tremendous blessing.

When I met the CEO of the company and described Karen's situation, she told me that her daughter experienced food allergies that caused much physical discomfort as well. However, she found a fabulous naturopath, Dr. Sie, who cleared her child of her food allergies by using NAET. She could eat those foods, symptom free, just twenty-four hours following treatment. I shared that I'd just learned of the technique myself but that my daughter was on a long waiting list for an appointment with someone else. But I intuitively knew that this doctor was the one I was looking for and that somehow we would get to see her right away.

I'll never forget that businesswoman looking into my eyes, mother to mother, saying, "This was why you *really* came to the meeting." She knew how synchronicity worked too. I felt such gratitude for this unexpected angel who came into my life and gave me the right information at the right time. It was plain to see that the Universe had brought us together for these brief moments for the desired, destined, and yet completely unex-pected exchange of information.

A little more than a week later, Karen was eating macaroni and cheese. No more elimination diets for my girl. This Heaven-sent doctor took her right in, used the technique, and cleared her of several allergies in just one visit. Dr. Sie eventually used other natural methods of healing that improved our whole family's health. As an added treasure, we have become close friends. I also consider her my mentor, as she further brought out the healer in me.

Just by being present during my children's healings, as well as by becoming Dr. Sie's patient myself, I learned about the real underlying causes of diseases and illness and how intention and energetic clearings can heal and prevent potential future issues. It opened my mind to the new wave of relatively unknown avenues of natural healing. All of these gifts had come from one simple and completely unexpected piece of advice from an absolute stranger.

The gifts are always there; it is a matter of paying attention, trusting, and taking the necessary action. As previously mentioned, I'm being strongly guided with this chapter. I wrote up to this point at least a month ago and then worked on other parts of the book. Something truly miraculous occurred yesterday that I knew would need to be expressed in this chapter.

Yesterday morning, I woke with the realization that my gold cross necklace wasn't around my neck. For twelve years, I've worn this piece of jewelry every day without ever taking it off, except for something like an x-ray. When I began my spiritual path and became open to the Heavenly dimensions, I felt I needed to always wear a symbol that showed I desired the presence of only the highest beings like Christ, those only of the light.

My first thought was that the chain had broken from all these years of constant use. I also thought this was one more reminder not to be attached to anything. So many of my belongings have been breaking down lately, an unusual number of things within a short period of time, and I knew these events were teaching me to release attachments. I found myself confronted with yet another test as my beloved cross, of all things, was missing. I checked my bedding twice, checked under the bed, and then the whole house—no cross. I knew it couldn't be lost and would eventually resurface, so I just let it go for the time being. That afternoon, I took my daughter to get her ears pierced.

Now I'm going to focus on specific details, and you'll see that when interpreting the meanings behind synchronicities, it is vital to be childlike in how you view things. When we explore and receive information as a child would, we allow ourselves to look outside the box. You may wonder why I'm making the specific connections that I'll describe, but I assure you that life is in the details. And when you pay close attention to details, you gain the clarity you desire. It's about being relentlessly aware while utilizing your intuition and feeling your way to a broadened understanding. Now that I've prepared you, let me continue with the story.

The lady who was to perform the piercing was getting the earrings ready, and for some reason, she mentioned that her father's office number and her cell number both included the number 404, the three numbers following the area code. She said, "It's really a *coincidence*." Karen and I weren't sure why she'd even brought up this obscure fact, and we wondered whether we'd missed something in the conversation. But then again, in our synchronistic world, there is purpose and meaning in most everything, even the obscure. Anyways, the fact that she said the word *coincidence* made me think that something was up.

She then said the total was $44.44. Well, you now know me: when number synchronicities occur, my antennae go up. This was a definite message that synchronicity was in high gear now, and as this woman pierced my daughter's ears, I could feel that more was ahead. Karen looked beautiful with her new sapphire stud earrings, and we decided to go to the bookstore for a while and relax and each curl up with a book.

After we parked, I noticed a car with the license plate "ANGEL." Here was another sweet sign that something was developing. As we walked to the bookstore, rain began to fall with large but few drops. Karen said, "A drop just went right in my eye." The same thing had happened to me, at the same time. I said, "It went into my eye, too! My left eye." It had gone into her left eye as well. I know this sounds so funny, but it was strange that raindrops would fall into both of our left eyes at the same time. I said, "It hit *the corner of my eye*."

We went our separate ways once inside the bookstore. Right away, I heard the name "Mary" repeatedly in a song playing from the store's overhead speakers. As I approached my favorite section of metaphysical titles, I was immediately drawn to two books. Time would soon show that it was significant that both books, *Archangels & Ascended Masters* and *Angel Visions*, were written by Doreen Virtue, PhD. I found a cozy chair next to Karen and sat down. When I opened *Angel Visions* right to a page with the headline "Mary Moved," it struck me: I'd encountered the name Mary again.

I believe that whenever you repetitively hear your name and from different sources, the Universe is trying to get your attention, and something is definitely up. The passage described a child's miraculous experience in church. This child saw, "out of the corner of my eye," the hands of the statue of the Virgin Mary move toward her and other children, who noticed the miracle as well. I made particular notice of the words *the corner of my eye*.

After browsing through Dr. Virtue's other book, which included information about archangels, I referred to the table of contents to find the
page where she writes about Archangel Michael. According to the text,
"The humans whom he enlists and works with are called 'lightworkers,'
and Michael asks them to perform spiritual teaching and healing work on
a professional or casual basis." My connection to Michael is described in
the chapter "The Angels among Us." This description, which I'd never
read before, fully resonated with me.

I also felt compelled to look up Kuan Yin, to whom I also feel connected. She is known as the Chinese Goddess of Compassion and, according to Dr. Virtue, "is often called 'the Mother Mary of the East'"—the
name Mary again. As I read this, I felt a presence—throughout my whole
body, a tingling feeling—and knew that the essence of Kuan Yin was with
me. I was then overcome with a certain knowingness. I told Karen I felt
that something miraculous was going to happen when we got home, some
kind of Divine sign.

When we returned home, I went right to my bedroom, and there on
the bed, on my white goose down comforter, was the cross! Part of me
thought that Scott had found it. He is the "finder" of the family; whenever
something is lost, he is usually the one that finds it. But a larger part knew
that this was the miracle I had anticipated. Actually, at the bookstore, I
had visualized that I would come home to find the cross around the neck
of one of my statues of Kuan Yin. I took the cross to Scott and asked
where he'd found it. He assured me that he had not.

After searching through my bed that morning and then making the
bed, I had seen no sign of my cross, and with my determined eyes, I would
have certainly seen it if it had been sitting on top of the bright white comforter. Also, I noticed that the cross was clasped and the chain unbroken
when I found it.

Given our three-dimensional reality, the chain would have had to either
break or unclasp itself to come off of me (the latter is much more unlikely,
because the clasp was very strong and had never done so before). There
was no rational explanation for the reappearance of my cross and its
still-clasped chain. This was indeed a miracle, and it was meant to be
shared with you, the reader!

Was it Kuan Yin? I believe so. In Virtue's book about archangels and
ascended masters, she writes that Kuan Yin is "devoted to helping us fully

open up to our spiritual gifts, attain profound knowledge and enlighten-ment, and reduce world suffering." I feel that Kuan Yin made her presence known to let me know that she is helping me in these areas, particularly while I am writing this book.

These kinds of experiences happen to many. I know someone who put on a necklace the right way, only to find it on backward without having touched it. I know someone whose cell phone rang with an important call when the phone was turned off. There are millions of examples of unex-plained occurrences. We can fruitlessly search for rational explanations for these events or just surrender to the beauty of being touched by those in the Heavenly realms.

I'm returning to finish writing this chapter, which seems to write itself.

Six days after my reunion with my cross, I met with Lillian, a former student of one of my spiritual development classes. Over lunch, I told her about my book and specifically about the cross miracle. When I started to explain what I'd experienced by referring to the Doreen Virtue books I'd read at the bookstore, she said that she listened to Dr. Virtue's CDs every morning and evening. Although it had been a few years since I'd read any of her books, up until just days ago, I shared that I had always admired her work and had considered taking one of her workshops. She said that she felt the same and that we should travel to one together, because workshops hadn't been held in Colorado.

After lunch, Lillian suggested that we go to the local metaphysical bookstore. Ironically, she had been wanting to buy another of Virtue's meditation CDs. I felt that Lillian was my messenger, so I bought some CDs as well. We went to the counter to purchase them, and the clerk mentioned that she was still in a daze following her powerful channeling experience the night before and apologized for being ungrounded. The woman described a vision of herself with an elephant and a crown. Strangely, she described in detail the gold crown, which came to points, with balls on top of each point. Had this woman not gone into such detail, I would not have made the connection.

The day before, my kids and I had gone to the Renaissance Festival. I told the clerk about my two most vivid memories from that day. One was seeing a gold crown, just as she'd described, with golden balls topping the

points; I'd found myself very attracted to it. Also, there had been a live elephant in the festival procession, and I'd been amazed at how it had walked
within five feet of us. The clerk knew that this synchronicity was signaling
something.

She went on to explain that after the channeling, which had been held
at the bookstore, she'd received a phone call late that evening. A man from
Tibet had called the store in search of a healer. I asked if she was a healer,
and she said she was a nonpracticing Reiki master. So she gave him someone else's name.

Completely surprised and with my voice raised, I asked, "A man from
Tibet of all places called this little bookstore in Colorado looking for a
healer?" To me, the message was obvious, but I know from experience that
messages can be hard to decipher when they're for you; sometimes we are
afraid to hear these messages. It was no coincidence that she'd answered
this phone call immediately following a profound spiritual experience. I
wondered why she wasn't practicing as a healer.

Oftentimes, we need to let each other figure things out—to allow
another to progress on his or her own path and not interfere—but I knew
that the synchronicity with the crown and the elephant indicated that our
meeting had been arranged through Divine intervention. I knew I must
speak up, even though I didn't even know this lady. So I told her, "All of
this is telling you that you need to work as a healer." She started to cry.
She knew it was true.

Months later, I returned to the bookstore, hoping to reconnect with the clerk
and see how she was doing. The manager of the store told me that this woman
was no longer working there but that she would take my phone number and
have her call me. When the woman contacted me just before this book went
into production, I was delighted to hear that she is indeed working as a healer,
feels she is exactly where she is meant to be, and even quit the bookstore job. I
shared that I was including this story in my book, and she told me that our syn-
chronistic meeting served as great validation for her.

It validated only what I'm sure she already knew deep down—it was time
to fully step into her passion and destined work. She said that a line of synchro-
nicities followed our meeting and that these signs further supported the same
message. She said that right after Lillian and I left, she'd picked a card from
none other than Doreen Virtue's Ascended Masters card deck. It was the card

*of the elephant-headed deity Ganesh, the popular Hindu god, and there was a
one-word message at the top of the card: "Yes."*

That evening I felt compelled to surf Dr. Virtue's website. I was
stunned to find that in six days she was going to be speaking in Fort Col-
lins, Colorado, and there were still tickets available. When I called Lillian
to tell her, she was shocked and very excited. We obviously needed to be
there.

On the day of the event, I had an appointment with a dermatologist.
For several days, I had been suffering with severe itching all over my body;
this itchiness had appeared out of the blue. The appointment could not
come soon enough, as the itching was becoming unbearable and affecting
my precious sleep. As the nurse wrote down my symptoms and physical
history, none other than "I Can See Clearly Now" came on the overhead
speaker. With a smile on my face, I cheerfully gave out the necessary background information. What I didn't know was that in minutes I would
clearly see what really had been going on behind the scenes recently.

The dermatologist came in and did a quick scan of the rash, which had
spread over much of my body. She said, "You're allergic to your gold
cross." I was overcome with emotion. The doctor thought I was upset
because I wouldn't be able to wear my cross anymore and began spouting
options. However, I teared up because I was deeply touched by the instant
recollection and understanding that I had been Divinely warned of this
allergy, when my cross suddenly went missing and then "magically" reappeared.

I had briefly considered the possibility that I was allergic to the gold in
my cross, but my desire to keep wearing it overrode the thought. Even my
children suggested that my cross might have disappeared because for some
reason I shouldn't wear it anymore. I didn't listen and suffered unnecessarily. Yet perhaps it's for the best, because I've learned once again how
unhealthy attachment is. I carry Jesus in my heart and don't really need an
outward symbol. I will listen better from now on. My cross is now placed
around my statue of Kuan Yin, where it will remain.

On the way to the Virtue event that night, I was excited to tell Lillian
about the further unfolding of the cross mystery. When we arrived at the
theater, just outside the doors was a sculpture of a buffalo that had the colors black, orange, and white. A butterfly was sitting on it, and Lillian

noticed that the butterfly's colors were the same as the colors on the sculpture. As soon as she mentioned that, the butterfly flew above her shoulder, then away from her, and then back and forth very fast seven times.

We had never seen a butterfly dart back and forth like that and we were amazed that it repetitively flew right to her shoulder. Usually, butterflies represent transformation, and buffaloes signify power. This event validated the new beginning that she was consciously aware of and confirmed that she was on the cusp of a powerful time in her life.

July 7, 2007 (07/07/07), was a powerful day for the earth and all its inhabitants. Many of us felt shifts on both personal and global levels on and around this day. I was guided to attend T.Harv Eker's "Seminar of the Century," which was being held that weekend in Snowmass, Colorado. Prior to leaving home for this event, I started to feel lower back pain, which has come and gone, especially in the past few years. It often progressed to the point where I couldn't stand up straight and had great difficulty going from a sitting to standing position. After thousands of dollars' worth of various treatments, nothing had provided healing or lasting relief.

I wondered how I would fare at the seminar, which was held outside at a ski resort and where much walking up and down steps and hills would be required. The night before the special day, I lay in bed and prayed with gratitude for my healing (a practice that will be discussed further in the chapter "Gratitude, Love, and Forgiveness Attract Miracles"). I specifically asked the angels to intercede and provide a miracle healing, as I sent white light from the crown of my head through my whole body and out my hands and feet. This is a practice I often use for healing on physical, mental, emotional, and spiritual levels.

I felt my angels' presence and was convinced that a healing had taken place. Yet the next morning I woke and found that my condition had *not* improved. Nothing was going to get me down on this day, though. After all, it was 07/07/07.

Following a morning of listening to motivational speakers, I was walking along the sides of the crowd, where vendors had set up booths. Halfway up the hill, I saw a practitioner working on someone's neck with a vibrating tool that looked to be providing deep massage. I had seen this booth the day before but thought it was promoting a conventional chiropractic adjustment—I was wrong.

Although I know that millions of people have been helped by chiropractic work, I was uncomfortable with receiving adjustments. Because of my rash judgment, which I'd made without getting the true story of the service this practitioner was providing, I had rejected the idea outright. This is a perfect example of how our expectations influence our perceptions, and then we either seek out proof that confirms our beliefs or just plainly dismiss any possibilities.

However, as I stood and watched the practitioner work on this day, I could feel it in my whole body that this was the answer to my prayers. My intuition was in high gear, moving me closer to the booth and prompting me to read the promotional material and speak with the assistant. It was explained that René-Claudius Schümperli, who created the AtlasPROfilax method and who trains specialists at his academy in Switzerland, discovered that the first cervical vertebra—the atlas, which carries the skull—is dislocated in practically every individual (for complete information, go to www.atlasprofilax.net). I intuitively knew, then and there, that my dislocated atlas was creating my back and hip issues.

According to the brochure, a single session utilizing this method would permanently align the atlas vertebra. Just one treatment? Could this be the miracle I'd requested, coming to me in an unexpected way? I followed the signs and feelings as another woman and I snatched up the last two appointments available that day.

That evening, the practitioner from Los Angeles sat me down, felt my neck, and immediately described just how dislocated my atlas was. "Of course you have lower back and hip issues," he said, and he further described how the dislocation was compressing my spinal cord. As soon as I stood up after receiving treatment, I noticed a foreign yet wonderful feeling. My shoulders were sitting back—effortlessly!

For as long as I can remember, I've had poor posture. Keeping my rounded shoulders back was very difficult. When I was ten years old, I wore a back brace, and although it corrected my main spinal issue over the few years that I wore it, my shoulder placement never improved. Suddenly, thanks to this new treatment, my shoulders were naturally sitting back and proper at the age of forty-six, for the first time that I can remember. I was delighted beyond words and noticed how good it felt to sit and stand straighter.

When I walked out of the booth, I realized that I no longer had pain in my lower back and hips. The pain was completely gone. I also found that my right leg, which has always been shorter, was now lined up perfectly with my left, heel to heel. People waiting for treatment noticed and commented on the smiling, bright-eyed girl bouncing out of the booth—me. After less than a half hour of treatment, the unexpected came into my life and provided a new beginning for my health. I felt reborn.

After having endured years of pain, thousands of dollars I'd spent on various treatments, many hours and hours of time for appointments that resulted in marginal and temporary relief, could it be that this one process, which requires just one brief follow-up session and weekly massage to support the healing process, had actually solved my spinal and hip issues? Anything is possible, and we should not believe in limitations. We are in the age of miracles! Miraculous alternative treatments and therapies are increasingly available.

It can take months to feel the full effects of this healing; I'm finding that it affects multiple areas of the body and all levels of being. I look forward to feeling even better and being graced with yet more positive changes. Had I not voiced a passionate request for healing and the cessation of pain, would I have allowed the unexpected to grace my life? Or would I have been stuck in my own perceptions, projections, and misbeliefs? I believe this healing was the very reason I was guided to attend the seminar.

When in the midst of pursuing my passion of writing this book, I received a gift that aided my physical vessel so I could act on my goals with wellness and good health. As my spine continues to straighten and readjust, so does the backbone and foundation of my purpose, and I am overflowing with feelings of gratitude.

I am deeply grateful for this opportunity to write and share my message with others. Throughout the writing of this book, allowing myself to expect the unexpected has been part of the creative process. I've let everything unfold in this new, untapped part of me, and this will result in a published book, which I have dreamed of for so many years. This surrender also yielded some near unbelievable synchronicities, most remarkably when my kids and I went to Michigan to visit family and friends in late July of 2007.

One morning, I was telling my parents about Carl Jung and how he believed in synchronicity and actually defined it for the world. A short while later, my son, daughter, parents, and I set off to have lunch in the quaint town of Frankenmuth, called "Michigan's Little Bavaria." After enjoying their famous family-style chicken dinner, my kids and I visited a store.

In one display were action figures of famous people including Jesus, Albert Einstein, Leonardo da Vinci, and—no, it couldn't be—Carl Jung! Of all the times I'd seen these displayed in various stores, I'd never seen the figure of Dr. Jung. There was just one left, and I decided to buy it, realizing it would be a great symbol to display on my desk.

When I found a Beatles T-shirt for my daughter, I approached the counter to purchase the shirt and Carl figure and handed the clerk my credit card. He said, "That will be $9.52." I told him that he hadn't rung up the T-shirt. In what seemed to be an attempt to correct the mistake— and it was the oddest thing—he began punching in several numbers, and I saw on the cash register a number that was nearly $1 million. I said with a laugh, "Wow, I don't think it's that much!"

He said he would void the transaction and then start over. Meanwhile, I saw on this first receipt the following:

Cash   949,460.00

Change due   949,450.48

At first I thought that he'd erroneously pushed the register buttons to *charge* me the huge six-figure amount. However, to my absolute delight, this "mistake" expressed that I had paid with nearly a million in cash! And I wasn't even paying in cash to begin with. Was it a mere coincidence that this extremely unusual occurrence happened when I purchased the Carl Jung figure, "Mr. Synchronicity" himself, versus all the thousands of purchases I've made in my life so far?

I asked the strangely unfazed clerk if I could keep the receipt (see photo). It would serve as a reminder of how I am indeed attracting wealth in my life. After being a stay-at-home mom for twelve years, and then a single mom, I am going to make it. Yes, this was a sign telling me so in the most perfect way, through the most fitting symbol of synchronicity: Carl

Jung, my hero. I wouldn't be surprised to learn that his spirit was with me on this day and was somehow behind this.

Looking closely at the receipt, I could not fathom how this could have happened. It is beyond understanding. Nothing like this had ever happened to me before. The new transaction was uneventful, and the clerk charged me the correct amount. Of course, I was quite excited for the rest of the day and am still overjoyed by the memory of what occurred.

When you expect the unexpected, you allow Heaven to shower you with magic, such as that described in this chapter. Throughout this book, I use the word *magic* to refer to events that are magical to us, through our level of understanding as humans. However, this magic is actually the natural state of our Universe.

Sometimes, Divine intervention comes in phases. Synchronicity may deliver the solution in pieces, like stepping-stones, for various reasons. When you're ready, the solution will fully present itself. Expect that it will indeed come, but don't bother wondering what the package will look like or who will deliver it. Just surrender to the gifts.

I surrendered to this chapter, not realizing what I would write. But as it turned out, Divine grace beautifully delivered the unexpected experiences—most of which occurred during the actual writing of this chapter—and thus the words.

```
        Frankenmuth Bavarian Inn
        713 S. Main Street
        Frankenmuth, MI 48734

          BAVARIAN INN WINE SHOP


Ticket#131942 Cus#OUR GUEST    Aug 01 07
Usr MMB        Rg# 52 Dr#521 Time 03:34
-----------------------------------------
Item Number        Qty   Price      Ext
-----------------------------------------
920727              1    8.98      8.98
ACTION FIGURE CARL JUNG

                        ---------------
Subtotal                          8.98
Tax                                .54
                        ===============
Total sale                        9.52


Cash                        949,460.00

Change due                  949,450.48
```

```
        BAVARIAN INN RESTAURANT
        713 S MAIN STREET
        FRANKENMUTH, MI 48734


        We are happy you are here!
        Thank you for shopping at
        Bavarian Inn's Market Platz!
```

CHAPTER 10

INTERPRETING SIGNS

*T*here are many ways to decipher the meanings of synchronicities in your life as they play out. One is by using a sign or dream dictionary to look up the specific symbol, such as an animal, a number, a color, an item, or an event. Another way is through meditation and asking for Divine help in determining significance. To me, the most natural and immediate way is through the limitless resource of intuition.

We all have that "gut feeling," which is intuition. Once you are aware of this innate ability and honor it, you can grow it. It may take time to get over self-doubts and the questioning of whether your imagination is playing tricks on you. If you make a promise to yourself to always honor and listen to this inner knowingness, your confidence will naturally build over time. You will realize that you were right on this occasion and that occasion, which will eventually grow into more advanced levels of intuition.

Intuition gives you wisdom, knowledge, peace, perspective, acceptance, understanding, and much more. It is both a vital and a most blessed part of the spiritual path. When connecting with your intuition, you immediately know whom to trust, whom not to trust, what products will nurture you best, what is harmful, when to act, and when not to act. Imagine having all your questions about health, relationships, career, finances, and other areas easily and effortlessly answered.

Right now, you can ask yourself a question, any question, and allow the answer to come. There is always a response! Make sure you are allowing it to appear. Just close your eyes, take a deep breath, and ask a simple question that would give a "yes" or "no" answer, such as "Will reading that book benefit me?" "Shall I sign up for this seminar everyone keeps telling me about?" or "Should I start buying organic milk?" Did the response come easily? Did you think it was your imagination? Did you trust it?

I enjoy consulting my favorite sign dictionary, *The Secret Language of Signs*, when deciphering various symbols, but I often need to use my intuition to guide me toward the direct personal meaning of the synchronicity. When I hit that skunk, which I told you about in the chapter "I Begin to Really See," the sign obviously meant that my thought "stunk." But signs aren't always that clear. Sometimes, they can be downright confusing.

Signs often carry specific personal meanings to individuals. If a person has an affinity for dragonflies, the dragonflies themselves may become an important sign for that person, whereas they have little or no meaning to another. I automatically know that certain signs, when they appear, are signaling something good for me, such as a synchronistic sighting of a hawk, a roadrunner, or a magpie. I have actually seen ladybugs inside the house in the winter, which I consider a very positive sign. Our angels know exactly what our favorite signs are.

The angels also know when we associate various signs to people in our lives, such as when we connect a song with a person. Whenever my friend Julie comes to town for a visit, it has somehow become a tradition to play and sing John Denver's "Take Me Home, Country Roads," on the way home from the airport. Because I associate that song with her, if I heard the song on the radio, at the moment a thought of her came to mind, I would consider that synchronistic. I would probably call to check on her or to seek out a message. Maybe my angels whispered the thought of her to me at that perfect time so that I would indeed call her for whatever reason.

From time to time, I also receive signs that present a challenge to me. When I have "garbage" synchronicities, I know there is something I need to clear out, whether they are misbeliefs, negative thoughts, or any baggage in my past that does not serve me. Let's say I'm obsessing with negative thoughts about a specific past experience. Just then, a garbage truck swerves into my lane, which gets my attention. I would consider that a sign that I must release the negative effects of that past occurrence. This type of sign is not to be feared but to be blessed, because the release is for my own highest good.

I was recently driving on the expressway behind a man who was behind a garbage truck. A small plastic bag flew out of the truck and right onto the man's rearview mirror, and, strangely, it stayed there for an unexpectedly long time, despite the high speed at which he was traveling. As I drove past the man, he opened the window and released the bag into the air while absorbed in conversation on his cell phone.

Although it was absolutely none of my business, I couldn't help but acknowledge the feeling that he needed to release some "garbage" out of his life but was oblivious to it. You may think I'm out of my mind to come up with this interpretation of such a simple occurrence. If so, you're absolutely right! I do go out of the confines of my "normal" mind, out of the box of everyday thinking, to decipher the language of signs. Perhaps the purpose of my taking notice of this event was to share that I do so. It also reminded me of a "garbage" synchronicity that a friend of mine experienced several years ago.

This friend was not an American citizen and had a green card. Out of the blue, I asked her if I could see what her card looked like. She went inside her purse to get it, and a look of panic appeared on her face. She realized that when she switched the contents from her old purse to a new one the day before, she had mistakenly thrown away her green card along with the old purse. When she returned home after our meeting, she found that her husband had already placed the garbage in the apartment complex's dump. In the end, they had to go through bags and bags of garbage before they found that card.

I thought it so odd that I'd asked to see her green card, but the words had seemingly come out of me without forethought—not a week later or a month before, but just when she needed to be alerted that she was about to lose an extremely important piece of identification. In addition, this synchronicity—which prompted her literally to go through garbage—was mirroring the need for her to go through her own "stuff," just as every one of us has to do from time to time. Indeed, soon after this occurrence, she was forced to confront some things that were holding her back.

When meanings behind signs are not so obvious, and when I'm not receiving an intuitive hit or am confused by it, I ask my angelic guides for wisdom concerning the synchronicities. When I do get a revelation, most commonly in the form of a thought, I always use discernment. I stay light and flexible to allow for further wisdom and understanding to flow forth. Sometimes, I can see only a little at a time. Maybe I am not ready for the full answer and need to trust that the layers of understanding will unveil themselves at the perfect time.

In whatever way I receive a meaning of a sign, I often confirm it with *muscle testing*, also called *applied kinesiology*. The body's intelligence provides answers to most any question by testing the responses of one's various muscles. In the last several years, the number of people using muscle testing for a variety of reasons has surged. Certainly, alternative health professionals of many kinds utilize this technique. More and more chiropractors muscle test to find out which parts of the body need adjustments. Even some conventional health professionals are, often quietly, jumping on board.

Muscle testing is used to answer any "yes" or "no" question or provide a "strong" or "weak" reading regarding health, relationships, work, and so on. Examples of possible questions are: "Is it in my highest interest to date Steve?" "Is Dr. Jones the best doctor for me?" or "Am I strong or weak to accepting this new job?" As long as the clear question can be answered with a "yes" or a "no" or can yield a "strong" or a "weak" reading, there are an infinite number of questions that can be asked.

The most common way to muscle test is for a person, the subject, to stand with his arm extended outward to the side. The tester asks the subject to resist the tester's pressure as her hand pushes down on the subject's arm. If the subject is holding in his other hand, say, a glass of milk, and the subject is actually allergic to milk, the subject's arm will weaken or fall to the side as the tester pushes down on his arm. But any muscle can be used for muscle testing.

When I demonstrated this technique on a friend, he was absolutely convinced that I would not be able to make his strong arm go weak, as this well-built man obviously lifted weights. With one arm straight out to his side, I asked him to touch with his other hand the point on his forehead where his eyebrows would meet—this is a polarity test that normally makes the muscles go weak. Sure enough, as I tested, his arm fell, much to his shock. So all you strong men out there, your body's inner smarts will indeed overpower your physical strength, and you can benefit from muscle testing as well. Many people enjoy being muscle tested, because they can actually feel their body's answers to the questions.

Years before I ever knew what muscle testing was, at the beginning of my spiritual path, I naturally started feeling sensations in my lips, one feeling for "yes" and another for "no." I would ask questions and feel the answer. Because I kept getting accurate answers, I knew the phenomenon was real even though I'd never heard of such a thing. It wasn't until just a few years ago that I learned about muscle testing and realized I'd been naturally practicing it all along; I'd just been using different muscles than those normally used.

I still feel the sensations in my lips, but I most often muscle test with my thumb and index finger. As mentioned, I test to confirm what my intuition reveals as the meaning of a sign. When in the grocery store, I use it to check how healthful or pesticide-free a product is. I muscle test what supplements are best for my children and me to take. As a healer, I intuit the underlying cause of someone's issues, which their subconscious is running on, and then muscle test to confirm my intuition. Then I explore what misbeliefs are holding this person back.

Throughout the writing of this book, I've relied mainly on synchronicity, intuition, and, beyond the rough drafts, muscle testing to validate that I've stayed on course to provide the best information I can. When I edit this material, I will muscle test to verify that the material is in line with my highest intention and purpose. I'll test whether I should add, remove, or clarify until I achieve the best results possible.

My intention is to write, with wisdom and integrity, the best book I can. I feel driven to get this message out as soon as possible. The first draft of this book was completed in just two months. I trust the process and the guidance I'm receiving, and that is why everything has fallen into place. Finding the right publisher, the right readers of the drafts, the right contacts, the right timing—all of these tasks have been easily and effortlessly accomplished, for the most part. Muscle testing confirmed what has naturally transpired.

Anyone can learn to muscle test. But muscle testing may not be for everyone. The tester must be of clear mind and heart and accepting of the answer. That is not always easy when asking questions, particularly with an emotional thread, about yourself or your loved ones. You can actually sway the answers with your own desires. So you need to be careful and willing to accept the truth and what is in your best interest. Also, you may receive a "yes" on something, only to find out that once you follow that direction, probably a direction you needed to initially follow to perhaps gain a fuller understanding or prove something to yourself, you get a "no." But it is always for good reason.

The bottom line here, again, is discernment. You must discern every answer. And you must listen to your intuition along with muscle testing, if you indeed choose to use this tool. Don't blindly follow the answers, especially when your gut is telling you otherwise. Make sure you verify that it's in your highest interest to test and that you are clear and able to receive accurate answers.

Sometimes an answer will seem downright crazy, but that doesn't mean it's necessarily wrong. It may offer a new way of looking at things or may be something that cannot be easily perceived with our human ways of understanding; if you feel the answer in your gut, though, it may need to be trusted or at least explored. The spiritual path may not be easy, but, in my opinion, there is nothing more fulfilling in life.

If you are so inclined, you can find more information about the styles and techniques of muscle testing by going online and googling the words *muscle testing* or *applied kinesiology*. You can easily learn how to check for polarity prior to muscle testing, to make sure that your answers will be accurate. If you know someone who muscle tests, you can ask this person to teach you in a matter of minutes—and then it just takes practice. Always be sure you are well hydrated when muscle testing. My favorite read on the understanding and benefits of applied kinesiology is Dr. David Hawkins's popular book *Power vs. Force*.

Many people I know use muscle testing in their daily lives, and I know several others who strongly feel it shouldn't be trusted, and I respect their opinions. I personally feel that this tool can be used very effectively—certainly when interpreting signs and in healing work—and I don't ever want to stop using it. But I always use it with discernment and responsibility. I sometimes notice people muscle testing in health food stores, in produce aisles, and while sitting with friends in coffee shops. Of course, maybe I'm visiting these places at the right time to notice, because like attracts like.

Allow me to share one vital practice I use in my work, as I learned it the hard way. I have found it imperative to *first ask if the question can indeed be asked*, especially when your gut feeling is telling you to refrain from asking.

If the answer is yes, then ask it. But if the question may invade another's privacy or if you're not ready for the answer, honor that. Or it may be about the future, and the future can always change. We can know only of potentials in our future because of our free will. So, if the question should not be asked for whatever reason, you must be aware that if you still ask it, you could receive the *wrong answer*. In that case, why bother?

I want to offer one more thought on intuition. It really is a form of channeling. The idea of sitting in an audience in front of a person who channels—who receives messages from archangels, ascended masters, and teachers from the Heavenly realms—may seem strange and downright scary. However, I believe that those gut feelings we get are an abbreviated form of channeling, whether from our higher selves, angels, or God.

As long as the channeler is receiving clear and honest messages from those of only light, the information should be celebrated and embraced, along with a healthy dose of discernment. Even the most well-intentioned channeler can retrieve imperfect information when deciphering the messages. But some of my most profound experiences, when I was farthest from feeling alone and most assured that I was walking my destined path, have occurred while witnessing live channeling sessions.

Just as we can tap into our intuition, we also have the ability to channel information from the Heavenly realms. These gifts are available to all of us; there are no exclusions here. For some, these gifts come naturally. For others, myself included, they require practice and experience to build confidence. Many of the greatest artists, inventors, and visionaries throughout history channeled their works. Present-day songwriters, authors, engineers, scientists, architects, teachers, and so on, also tap into the Universal "pipeline" for their creative pursuits.

As we evolve, we receive more gifts, and it is becoming much easier for all of us to receive and interpret Divine messages. We internalize the tools, and they become part of our natural way of being. They allow us to live more purposefully, authentically, creatively, and healthfully. We interpret meaning in our lives, often through the gift of synchronicity, as spiritually beings living in human bodies.

*   *   *   *

I cannot stress strongly enough that you must diligently and regularly verify that all messages of guidance come from only the highest source. There are beings who resonate at lower vibrations in the etheric realm, just as there are those human beings on earth who hold more negative energies. Your pure intention, absent of fear, to work with those only of the highest vibrations of light will make it so.

CHAPTER 11

THINGS AREN'T ALWAYS
WHAT THEY SEEM

O nce we embrace synchronicity, we seek meaning in all events. Our experiences with it push us to see things in new ways, from a higher perspective, and with an open mind. We look beyond the surface, because we learn quite quickly that things aren't always what they seem.

When I began to meditate, earlier on my spiritual path, I learned to focus my awareness, with my eyes closed, on the space between the eyebrows; what is referred to as the *third eye*. As you may know, this is where one receives clairvoyance. Soon after I learned to access information in this way, during a period of time, I kept seeing a baby when in meditation.

A vision of a sweet infant would come into focus for about three full seconds, as if I were watching a black-and-white television screen, and then the image would fade away. This happened on several occasions, including in my dream life. I thought it was a preview of a new arrival in my family, and that caused discomfort within me. My marriage wasn't secure, and I already had two beautiful children and did not desire to bring a third one into our lives.

I also noticed an increased attraction to the color orange. Although I'd always dressed in understated colors, I suddenly felt a strong desire to wear orange and purchased a couple of new orange tops. I didn't understand what either of these symbols truly meant, nor did I make any kind of connection between them.

After a few months of trying to decipher the meanings of these signs, I shared this information in a synchronistic meeting with someone who seemed to know a lot about dream meanings. She said that a baby represented new beginnings. The color orange symbolized the same thing.

About a year later, in June 1999, my family and I moved to New Mexico, which created an incredible new beginning for us. We flourished there in so many ways, and, for all of us, it truly and immediately felt like home. New Mexico offered an exciting and casual style of living that reflected my personality. More importantly, it marked a new beginning for my spiritual path. So the lady was right about the meanings behind the baby and the color orange. It was a powerful message that things aren't always what they seem. Sometimes, things are meant to be taken literally, and other times they are not.

Practicing relentless discernment is vital on the spiritual path and the search for meaning behind synchronicity. This was illustrated most clearly to me when I kept receiving scary signs that someone in my life was going to die. Years went by before I understood that the person was dying energetically, not physically, but ended up rebounding and being okay. I shared this with a friend who experienced similar synchronicities about someone in her life, but this death, too, was on an energetic level. Things aren't always what they seem, and this is why throughout this book I stress the importance of discerning all messages.

The same method applies when we explore present life issues that we find are actually mirroring issues in our past lives. We carry our traits and talents from our previous lives into our present incarnations. We also bring along memories of our pain and trauma at a cellular level until we can release them from our subconscious. So, what you are feeling or experiencing may have nothing to do with your present reality. There are many ways to achieve these healings from past lives, and your intention will surely attract the best vehicles to you.

As a hypnotherapy student, I sought answers as to why I was having trouble losing weight. Under hypnotic trance, I regressed to a past life as a boy in India, where I was starving and was the last of my family to die from famine. I reexperienced the moment of death; I was utterly joyous, thanking God for ending my suffering. Immediately after that, I went to my next incarnation as a woman in France. I was sitting in a chair and feeling extremely sad, and I was the largest woman I had ever seen. Obviously, I'd made sure in that lifetime that I would have plenty to eat and never starve again.

In this life, I am somewhere in the middle of the road—not morbidly obese, far from emaciated, and definitely overweight by varying degrees throughout much of my life. I have needed to clear the memories of these past lifetimes, and I have also worked on a new challenge recently.

Fat is a buffer to negative energies. As an intuitive healer, I have subconsciously added fat to my body to prevent the absorption of negative energies from others, those energies that they are releasing for their healing. Since childhood, I had been empathic, identifying with and even taking on others' hardships and feelings as my own. It took me all these years to learn to protect myself, to achieve a delicate balance while still showing empathy and compassion to others.

I achieved a fuller awareness of this recently at a healing workshop. The teacher was talking about how some use fat to protect themselves from others' energies during healing work. She said, "See this?" as she poked her fingers all over my stomach and hips. "This isn't Mary!" she said. I felt like a ball of bread dough that she was kneading. "This is other people's stuff that she has taken on as a healer."

She went on to explain that I needed to learn to always clear myself of other people's negative energies and to stop using fat as a buffer. This woman was right. I finally made the connection that when working on something significant for someone, in my personal life especially, it would cause me to feel an overwhelming hunger and put on weight. Aside from healing work, it would make sense that one can also, unknowingly, add unwanted fat to their bodies by being an empathic friend, family member, or parent.

My own situation has made me especially sensitive to others with weight problems. Things are going on subconsciously that shouldn't be judged. It's easy to say, "Oh, they just love food too much and cannot control themselves." However, our subconscious controls us—it runs our hunger levels—and unless we tackle our deep-rooted issues from our present lives or from previous lifetimes, we can allow ourselves to become victimized by them through our lack of awareness.

Carl Jung said it best: "Until you make the unconscious conscious, it will direct your life and you will call it fate." We have the power to reprogram the software of the subconscious (or unconscious) through many methods including energy work, hypnotherapy, and other alternative modalities, as well as affirmations, working with our angels, meditation, and prayer. It all begins with awareness and acknowledgment. As an even greater challenge, our pain is often caused by things we have no control over.

I admire the bold message in Jewel's song "Pieces of You." This song explores the judgments people make based on one's looks, sexual orientation, and race. The lyrics, as I interpret them, shed light on the hatred some feel for that which we cannot control. The song asks if one hates "'Cause he's (she's) pieces of you?" This is a brilliant song, written by someone so young at the time, and yet so wise.

As mentioned before, it is said that if we feel hatred toward a race in one lifetime, we may reincarnate as a member of that race in the next life and will experience the loathing we once felt toward others. It is karmic retribution—what goes around, comes around.

This points to a whole additional level of "pieces of you." Of course, as souls, we choose to incarnate into many different challenging situations—for example, our geographic location, our physical or emotional problems, or the color of our skin. Again, not everything is about karma; we also preselect challenges that will help us grow our souls and raise our vibrations.

Since I was a child, I've thought that when we get to Heaven, we must look on prejudice as the most puzzling thing. As spirits, I imagine one telling another, "I can't believe I judged you by the color of your skin. Why on earth was one color better than the other? That is the silliest thing." On top of it, we aren't even our bodies, our skin, or our looks—none of it. And we're changing our bodies, our skin, and our looks every lifetime anyway!

Because we have all been male and female in past lifetimes, I wonder if same-sex attraction could be at least somewhat caused by one's last incarnation; for instance, if a woman who's attracted to men, returns as a man, he may still be attracted to men. As souls, we are male and female. As human beings, we have varying degrees of both male and female energies within us. When we look at things with new eyes and new perceptions, we see that discrimination of any kind is unwarranted and unjust. What if, over our many lifetimes, we have been all of it—thin, fat, healthy, sickly, black, white, gay, straight, wealthy, and poor? Thus, one's hatred of others could be mirroring the hatred of one's self.

When I think about politics, the global scene, and deeply upsetting and horrifying situations like war, the only way I can stomach them is to say to myself, "Maybe things aren't what they seem." Looking at the world from a higher perspective, I consider the possibility that these awful and destructive events are actually happening so that we get shaken up. When we wake up and demand peace, anything that speaks of hatred, greed, corruption, and deception will no longer be tolerated. The darkness actually causes us to command more light. What if this is what it takes?

We *are* entering a new age of peace, even though it may not *seem* so. This is also why so much negativity is coming up: to fight the positive energy that is pervading. It is one last, final hurrah. Like attracts like, and what we focus on expands. As we focus on peace and not on war, turmoil, and unrest, we create peace. It is law. And peace is imminent.

This is why the Indigo children are here. They are those highly sensitive, wise, and intuitive beings who've incarnated within the last two to three decades to make a difference in the world. These nonconforming, independent children are filled with integrity. They are rebelling in order to create positive change, knowing they each have an important mission to accomplish and will assume roles, as they grow up, that allow them to complete those missions. Many are diagnosed as having ADD (attention deficit disorder) and ADHD (attention deficit/hyperactivity disorder), but there is significant concern coming from various sources that these kids are being mislabeled.

In more recent years, the Crystal children, also spiritually gifted, have and continue to incarnate. These extremely sensitive, loving, and telepathic beings are leading us into a world of love, truth, and peace, purely by their example. Like the Indigos, they have clear, intense, and wise eyes. So if you don't believe we are indeed moving toward a Heavenly earth, take notice of these children.

The new children are known by other names as well, but what is important is that we are aware of and celebrate their uniqueness and support them in every way we can. They have different ways of learning and being, and their sensitivities can be overwhelming. Their paths are not easy ones. The more we understand them and help ease them through their own challenges, the better we can help them fulfill their grand purposes. I highly recommend two reputable websites to attain further information regarding these children: www.indigochild.com and www.childrenofthenewearth.com. The human species is indeed evolving.

When we look at things from a higher perspective, we allow for a deeper understanding of the way things really are, and who each of us really is, which will help usher in our world's new beginnings.

CHAPTER 12

RELEASING FEARS

*I*n the movie *Defending Your Life*, starring the hilarious Albert Brooks and the amazing Meryl Streep, their characters die and go to this place between Heaven and earth called Judgment City. There they are basically on trial to defend their lives. Various times when they felt fear in their life experience are observed in a courtroom setting. If they were deemed worthy to go on, they would, but if it was decided that they hadn't overcome their fears, they would have to reincarnate back to earth. I'd never learned so much from a comedy.

Fear is what mostly holds us back in life. Of course, some fear is necessary to keep our risks reasonable and to protect ourselves. Like with everything else in life, balance is key. Are your fears natural, and are you still able to act in spite of them? Or are they paralyzing you? If your answer is the latter, you may be cheating yourself of your potential growth on this earth and not achieving your purpose. It is said that courage is having fear and still moving forward despite it.

Life is challenging enough without having outside influences making it harder on us. The media, in particular, increases our fears in so many ways. When you watch, especially, or read the news to learn about global events, you, along with tens of millions of other people, cannot help but focus on the mostly negative information. This builds and breeds fear. Of course, our intentions are honorable: to be responsible, aware, and well-informed citizens.

However, when millions of people focus on the tragedies—on the upsetting and arguably slanted stories—we unknowingly perpetuate the negativity in our reality purely by focusing on it. Even though we are distressed and upset about what we are hearing and passionately wish for change, the focus is still on the negative. If it's true that what we focus on expands, are we not expanding the negativity? This is distressing. How do we stay responsibly informed citizens with often-skewed negative news and yet remain positive?

On the other side of this coin, the news actually mirrors the darkness to such a degree that it causes us to demand the light. If we weren't so heavily exposed, perhaps we wouldn't get as shook-up and demand drastic change. Looking at things from a higher perspective can often seem contradictory. But the bottom line is that we stay in constant touch with what is best for each other, on all levels, and stay on top of our true intentions for this world as well as ourselves.

You cannot turn on the television these days, in the United States, without being subjected to a deluge of pharmaceutical ads. I firmly believe that watching these commercials is very dangerous for our health. All the words about diseases and symptoms are being repetitively heard by our subconscious as well as our conscious minds. We are told about an endless number of medications as if we cannot live without them. Of course, some medications may be necessary and are to be blessed, but should a large percentage of us three hundred million plus Americans be bombarded on a daily basis with these messages?

We are being inundated with the energy of disease. Whether we sit idly in front of the television or walk through the store that promotes foods that prevent this or that disease, even without paying specific attention, our subconscious minds are still recording everything. We must counter these influences by concentrating on and feeling gratitude for our health and what is working well in our bodies.

These influences are what I call "fear pollution," and whenever I'm around it, I use my intention to reverse it. Along with the power of my imagination, I say or think the reverse, such as "All is peaceful," "All is well," or "All are healed." I limit reading and, especially, watching the news and reduce my exposure to fear pollution in any way I can. If I see and hear part of a pharmaceutical television ad before I'm able to mute it, I say, "Healthy," or I laugh at how silly the ad sounds, when the potential side effects described appear to greatly override the benefits.

Yes, laughing the ridiculousness away is a healthy option. I know that if I ever really do need a particular medication, I don't need a television commercial to inform me of its existence—that's what doctors are for. I don't need pharmaceutical companies constantly planting ideas in my mind. I imagine a world that understands that we create our own realities—a world in which messages that, for monetary profit or political gain, irresponsibly create fear are no longer "beaming out."

When we allow ourselves to get trapped into fear and focus on it, we can actually attract and thus create synchronicity that reflects that fear. So, if you're getting signs that reflect something negative, you need to discern by asking yourself if the signs are reflecting reality or your illusion of fear.

Being a single mom with kids can potentially elicit all kinds of fears. The worst time is during the night, when I sometimes wake up gripped by fear. When I was a teenager, a psychic told me that I didn't sleep well because I worry too much, which was absolutely true. When I go into that "worry state," he said, I should just give my problems to God. When I followed his advice, it worked. Along with my worries, I released a huge weight off my shoulders. It was a very freeing practice, but I lacked the discipline to regularly maintain it.

I still release my worries, but I use my own newly created visualization technique that makes the practice much easier to sustain, especially when I'm trying to sleep. When I allow myself to be consumed with fears from time to time, I visualize a box above me. I send my worries right to the box, to God, knowing He will take care of them. I see them going out of sight. When I'm having one of those "worry marathons," I just send those fear-based negative thoughts, one by one, to the box.

As soon as I catch myself with yet another worry, off it goes to the box so I can return to sleep. Of course, I wish I could say I do this flawlessly, but that is not so. However, the more I practice, the more I remember to do so, and the more I choose to live in a state of love rather than fear. That's what I expect of myself: to continually improve and to be a better creator.

As I edited the previous paragraph, Tracy Chapman's song "Hard Wired" came on from the random shuffle of my iTunes. I didn't make the connection until the words "We've got a box to put in your brain" were sung.

Of course, sending worries to the box may be just a temporary solution to help me sleep or to stop useless mental chatter when I'm involved with other things. Eventually, that which I can control and change will need to be dealt with. The best way I have found to confront these issues is to imaginatively throw love and light on them, with appreciation to God for His help. This simple practice of surrender gives me an immediate sense of peace while opening the door to miracles.

I am most grateful to have attended live channelings of the angelic entity Kryon through Lee Carroll at many different meetings and conferences. Kryon initially taught and convinced me that we each have the ability to send light, purely through intention, to dark places anywhere in the world. "Don't send your ideas or thoughts … just the light. The metaphor is that you're illuminating dark places so that others may have free choice and see or discover hidden ideas that may contain solutions for some of the biggest problems on Earth" (*In The Spirit Online Magazine*, Q & A, www. kryon.com). This practice opened my heart and mind to the endless possibilities.

What can you shine Divine illumination on in your own life? Think of some issue you have that seems unsolvable. Perhaps it has to do with your spouse, your work, or your financial situation. Be sure to surrender the worries, anxieties and pressures that this issue has caused—fully intend to let them all go and release the charge—by sending them to the box.

Now, with the incredible power of your imagination, visualize love and light shining right through the box that is holding your issue. Then infuse feelings of gratitude into a statement such as "Thank you, God (or Spirit, Universe, higher self, etc.) for shining love and light on _____." Trust that Divine intervention will occur, with your complete and necessary release.

With this practice, you, as a co-creator, have now set into motion a solution. You will find the answers to your situation illuminated by the Universe. You don't need to know the details and should not be attached to any particular outcome; this may prevent you from allowing the Divine to show you something you may not have imagined. Just allow the answer to unveil itself in its own perfect time and relax into the feelings of peace and acceptance, now that you have loosened and released the grips of fear, worry, and frustration.

Synchronicity will step in to present the wisdom that you require. The answers will emerge through the people who suddenly come into your life, or the opportunity you would never have imagined will make its appearance known. Sometimes it's a light bulb that goes on and causes you to shift your thinking or the paradigm you operate from. Remember that although problems sometimes fix themselves or are touched by God's grace, they usually require your taking action.

Realize that love and light repel the darkness wherever you shine them with your intention. Be aware that this act may bring up negativity only so that it can be healed and then released. Watch your reactions if something challenging comes up, so that you acknowledge it as a blessing and then follow through.

Once you perform this technique, you will find the act of shining love and light indeed miraculous. You will realize how powerful you are as a co-creator. You will find that you can shine love and light wherever you need them in your life.

Shine love and light on your relationships, your job, your home, your mental chatter, your low energy, your depression, your bank account, your confusion, your frustrations—any issues that you may have. Imagine shining love and light on someone you care about who is sick, grieving, lonely, or suffering from an addiction. The best way to help loved ones is to send them this powerful energy rather than taking on their hardships, which only deplete you, energetically, on mental, emotional, physical, and spiritual levels.

Fear is the polar opposite of the love that we are as spiritual beings. As we release fears, we connect best to who we really are and live from that state of being. We show trust in God.

CHAPTER 13

WHAT WE FOCUS ON EXPANDS

When we focus on what we don't want, we keep attracting that which we don't want. Truly, we create exactly what we don't desire. In other words, if we focus on ridding ourselves of undesirable weight, we keep focusing on the excess weight itself, which creates continued extra pounds. If we focus on how we don't want certain people in our lives, they are in our lives more profoundly than ever. If we focus on how difficult life is, we get a difficult life.

Also, if we focus on wanting something, that's what we attract, "wanting" whatever that is. Ours is a literal Universe, one that requires that we choose our thoughts, feelings, words, and actions with great care. When we intend something as if it has already manifested, we actually create in a most desirable manner. *Choose* to have a happy life, as if you are already living it, but don't *want* a happy life. The act of wanting something is not in line with the powerful being that you are.

To prove to yourself how your focus on any one thing will create it in your life, try the following experiment. Pick some item that you don't regularly see or hear about in everyday life, such as a compass or a unicorn. As often as you can think to, focus your mind on that object for a period of at least one day. Then, watch it synchronistically come into your awareness in some way, through a sighting, in someone's speech, or through the written word.

For instance, say you focus on an antique typewriter, a yellow marble, or a blue moon. You'll marvel at the magic when you see the words *old typewriter* in the new book you're reading, find a yellow marble next to a curb, or overhear someone say, "Well, once in a blue moon ..." If you aren't aware of anything showing up, then continue to focus.

I learned the hard way to focus more on the positive than on the negative in my life. For instance, when I had a run of miserable service experiences—with my car, appliances, and banks, one after another—it took me a while to understand that I was unwittingly creating these bad experiences on a subconscious level, which culminated in a significant life lesson.

One awful situation would upset me, and I would then focus on the negative, on exactly what I didn't want—poor service. I would complain to family and friends, saying, "You won't believe what happened *now!*" I would relive the experience again and again in my mind and allow the frustration and angst to build, and then the bad situation would end up repeating itself with a new face, a new service, and, in the end, more frustration. After drudging through these negative experiences, I finally got it. I needed to bless these happenings as my teachers and change my thoughts, feelings, words, and actions.

Even though I eventually understood what was going on behind the scenes, that understanding, alone, wouldn't bring an end to my run of challenges. Whenever I moved toward mastery of a life lesson—such as this one, that we create our realities—I would then find myself being spiritually tested. For example, if someone provided me with poor medical service that caused me harm—something much more serious than, say, inept car service—that would be an ultimate test of how I would carry my thoughts and reactions. It would also be that practitioner's test regarding providing more responsible medical care.

The Law of Attraction brings together just the right people and the right experiences for deep spiritual reasons that we may not be consciously aware of. We all experience both of these types of challenges; not only through what we attract with, primarily, our thoughts and feelings but also through what we attract in the way of necessary spiritual tests for our growth.

It's impossible to be human and never think negatively. When I struggle, obsessing with negative thoughts, I send them to "the box" and send the issues love and light (as described in the previous chapter). I then turn my focus onto that which I do choose: quality service and, better yet, quality products. "I love how my car runs so well." "Refrigerators seem to last forever." "I feel so blessed that things come so easily and effortlessly." I use the words *easy* and *effortless* as much as I can; they counter all those times when I mindlessly chose *difficult*.

For any of you who feel powerless, deprived, or depressed or who have mindlessly chosen *difficult*, I suggest that you find one thing that you are really happy with in your life. Let's just say you have a dog, and you really love your dog. Be in that place where you experience wonderful feelings about your dog, and let the appreciation for that being flow. Focus on the gratitude you feel for the presence of your dog in your life and the unconditional love it gives you. This simple practice makes you feel great and more joyful, and it will attract more of the same feelings this dog provides. It may attract someone that offers unconditional love, or perhaps another dog will find you and give double the joy.

Then think of something else—a family member, a friend, your garden, or even a piece of music—and do the same thing. Flood your being with feelings of gratitude, and I guarantee you, if you were feeling down, you won't anymore. Gain awareness of the many things you feel grateful for, and soon you will find that your life is actually abundant and joyful. If you get a negative thought or a feeling of lack, or a feeling of "Yeah, *that's* wonderful, but *this* isn't," just say to yourself, "cancel, cancel," and stay in the positive flow. Watch for the blessings that will continue to manifest. And when they do, fully acknowledge them, no matter how "small" they are, and bathe them in gratitude. Never taking anything for granted!

By practicing this way of looking at things in our own lives, we eventually acknowledge that what we focus on does indeed expand. We then step into our true power and recognize who we really are—spiritual beings only pretending to be humans. I dared myself to make that step a couple of years ago, when we lived nearly two miles away from a small body of water that was nicknamed "Stink Lake." It emitted hydrogen sulfide gas, which produced an offensive rotten-eggs odor. When my kids and I drove by the lake, we were shocked to see that the water was purple. At one point, the smell permeated the house we'd just moved into.

When I realized that the energy of the lake needed to be changed, I stood by the water and renamed it "Rose Lake," for I imagined it smelling beautiful, like a rose. I energetically cleared and strengthened it, purely with intention, and focused on it being a healthy body of water. After that day, we never once smelled the bad odor again. Did the negative energies from understandably frustrated residents and their references to it as "Stink Lake" cause the water to reflect those energies—because what we focus on expands? Did the smell suddenly go away because the county was treating it over time? I cannot prove any of this to you, but I believe that after several weeks of emitting that odor, "Stink Lake" truly became "Rose Lake" once it was filled with positive energy.

This presents a significant question regarding our most precious resource. Can water be changed with our intentions, words, thoughts, and prayers? Just refer to Dr. Masaru Emoto's books and experiments (including what happens when people collectively pray on large bodies of water), as referred to briefly in the chapter "Nature Speaks," for the answer.

What if people collectively pray on a cure for a specific disease by seeing it bathed in love and light? What if the energetic reaction to that practice allows a pioneering scientist or group of scientists to tap into that place that geniuses such as Einstein, Edison, and Leonardo da Vinci have accessed, and the breakthrough cure is discovered? Do we dare be that powerful?

On a personal level, as you're walking through the grocery store, driving on the highway, or sitting in a restaurant, you can send love and light to strangers. Of course, all your friends, even your mate, were once strangers. Feel and imagine love and light coming from your heart and beaming outward to others. On some level, they will feel and benefit from the loving energy. You will feel blissful. It feels so good to do something so positive and quiet and yet so powerful. What goes around comes around, and you will create for yourself what you send outward to others.

CHAPTER 14

GRATITUDE, LOVE, AND FORGIVENESS ATTRACT MIRACLES

When my son, Scott, was in first and second grades, he needed extra help in both speech and reading. Although he was a very bright young boy, something wasn't clicking in his mind when it came to making connections with words. During his second-grade year, every night before going to sleep, he prayed with gratitude: "Thank you, God, for helping me to read and speak better."

After practicing this for a few months, his situation dramatically improved. He no longer needed special help. I recall it as if it were yesterday when his reading teacher said to me, "I have never seen such improvement in all my years of teaching. I call Scott my 'Miracle Boy.' You must have been working really hard with him." But the truth is, I really wasn't. What this teacher didn't know, until I later told her, was that Scott prayed with gratitude for what he wanted, as if he had already been graced with it; this practice allowed the miracle to appear. It was a remarkable happening for a little guy.

When I wanted to sell my home a year ago, there was no logical indication that it would sell easily. A house down the street, of a similar size and style, had been on the market for over a year. Several comparable homes in the subdivision had been listed for many months, and nothing was moving. Prior to my purchase of this house, it had been on the market for two six-month periods. My real estate agent told me to just be glad if I got out of the subdivision and not to be picky on an offer. These facts did not matter, because I was determined to sell this house quickly and for a fair market price. I knew that I would receive an acceptable offer in two weeks, and I thanked God as if it had already happened.

I told my agent I would receive an offer on the home in two weeks time, and she said that this goal wasn't at all rational, but because she was also a person with a metaphysical background, she expressed confidence in me. Soon after I put the house up for sale, a nice couple came in for a viewing. We spoke for a while and found we had much in common. I mentioned that we'd moved to Colorado from New Mexico. She asked where in New Mexico. I told her the name of the small town, but, for some reason, I said it with the proper Spanish accent, although I never say it this way to non–New Mexicans. "Plah-cee-tahs," I said. She responded in shock: "Plah-cee-tahs?! My mom lives there, and I want to move back to New Mexico. I miss it."

Just before their arrival, I had been looking at a New Mexico realty website, fantasizing about moving back and living in an adobe home. I shared this with her. This was just one of the many synchronicities between us that we discovered within a short conversation. I knew when these people walked out the door that I'd just sold my house and that they were to be the buyers. Synchronicity itself unveiled that knowingness. A week went by and my agent had not heard from them; however, I never wavered in my belief, convinced that I would receive an acceptable offer within the window of time that I'd declared.

Exactly thirteen days after my house was put on the market, my agent called and said, "Well, you're one day early, but that couple you liked put in an offer for the house." When I went into the realty office to sign on the fair offer, the support staff that I had come to know told me they had laughed when they heard my prediction that I'd get an offer in two weeks. They weren't laughing anymore. They were amazed and wanted to know if I was a psychic.

The bottom line is, I just knew it would happen, and I intended it with much gratitude, as if it had already happened. It didn't matter that others thought I was being irrational, that homes hadn't been moving in the sub-division, or that there were fourteen hundred other homes up for sale in that city. It was a done deal.

Someone in the coffee shop where I'm writing just said, "Well, someone has to buy that property" and continued to talk about real estate. This constant mirroring of what I'm writing about validates that I'm in alignment with my work.

We co-create our miracles by praying with gratitude and knowing with-out a doubt that what we desire will come to fruition. If doubt seeps in, which happens much more easily with adults than with young children (we've been away from the spirit world much longer than they), the progress or appearance of a miracle can be hampered. If you believe you are not worthy of receiving miracles, then that is exactly what you'll get, "not worthy of receiving miracles."

Practice asking with gratitude for what you desire. You can begin by saying, "Thank you, God, for ..." or "I am deeply grateful for ...," and really get your feelings behind it. If this is new to you, I suggest experi-menting with something small, whether tangible or not, if that feels more comfortable. Speak the words, feel the gratitude for receiving what you desire, and fully expect it to appear in your life. This will set the tone for your overall growing abundance.

There's a reason that we keep hearing from so many teachers and authors about how important it is to show constant gratitude. People who live with full, heartfelt appreciation for all they have are creating joyful and abundant lives. Being an eternal optimist, filled with gratitude, is the best way to create an optimal life, for one's self, for others, and for the world.

When my kids were younger, we kept a running gratitude list on a large chalkboard in our kitchen. I saw firsthand how this breeds positive energy into daily family life. The list naturally evolved to the behavior of verbally expressing our appreciation and truly living from that state of mind. Mod-eling the art of gratitude for your children is a beautiful and beneficial action for all involved. It will bind your family even closer, especially when you find that what you are most grateful for is each other.

This practice will also increase the positive flow of good things toward your family. When children learn this type of behavior from a young age, they grow up to become joyful, positive, and powerful adult beings. Get your kids into the gratitude habit! Children are at least as powerful creators as we are, and, well, that is a whole other book.

I highly recommend finding a "gratitude buddy," whether it's your child, mate, friend, or co-worker. Every day, you agree to e-mail or call each other to present a rundown of what you are grateful for that day; if your gratitude buddy is a family member, you, of course, can share your feelings in person. Speaking or writing your thoughts of appreciation makes you focus on the positive things in your life, and in each others lives, which will bring more of the same. You help each other to stay on course. When two or more are gathered, powerful things happen.

Having a gratitude buddy can become a contagious thing. Together, you and your buddy may end up creating a "gratitude circle" as you continue to explore the gratitude phenomenon. You can even hold monthly meetings where you focus on gratitude and inspire each other, sharing success stories of how you're creating a better life. The focus should be personal at first, because helping the self puts you in a better position to help the world collectively. Then, as a group, you can focus on things such as global peace, food for all beings, a healed environment, cures to diseases, and changing adverse weather conditions. This is how gratitude can create miracles in the most profound and monumental ways. A gratitude circle is actually a co-creation circle, because you are coming together to create with God through the power of gratitude. Making children part of your circle would be especially grand.

This is what the song "Let There Be Peace on Earth" means, as it goes on to say, "And let it begin with me." Except, it's everything: peace, health, sustenance, abundance, joy, freedom, and so on. We start by manifesting these things within ourselves, and making ourselves whole, which causes us to become stronger and increasingly aware of our abilities to create. We then gather and create a better world and make it whole, as well. Do we dare be that powerful?

Are we so powerful that we can even create more synchronicity in our lives? As I stressed previously, synchronicity is always there; it is simply a matter of whether we are aware of it. We must first increase our awareness of it. Are we listening to the stranger in the department store or the song on the radio? Are we really aware of the sign on the billboard, the bird that flies in front of us, or the book that falls off the shelf for no explainable reason? And then, are we making the necessary connections? Once we become aware of the magic, we express gratitude for synchronicity. When we focus on synchronicity with feelings of appreciation, we attract even more of it—it's as simple as that.

Whenever I experienced synchronicities with the song "I Can See Clearly Now," which directed the writing of this book twelve years later, I would get so excited each time. My heart would fill with gratitude that I was being guided and presented with such magical moments. I realized that the more I got excited and felt grateful for these moments—and believe me, they were genuine feelings—the more often synchronicity would show itself.

The act of pointing out and sharing synchronicities with others also creates more synchronicity. You become an impetus for others' awareness, just as this book is hopefully inspiring you, the reader. I believe that I've experienced a record number of synchronicities during the writing of this book not only so that I would receive the validation but especially so that I would share my experiences with you.

I remember telling my friend, Ann, from Michigan about the 444 phenomenon. About a year later, when visiting friends and family there, she and I went out for dinner. After we ate, we got in the car, and she said she had been looking for 444 all this time but hadn't seen it.

When I pulled out of the parking space as we were talking, I passed a parked car that had 444 on its license plate. The car was backing out as I exclaimed, "We just passed a car with it!" Ann didn't believe me, so I circled around to catch up with the car to prove it to her. Just as the car came back into view, it drove past another parked car with 444 on its license plate as well. We laughed and laughed, along with the angels, I'm sure. Had we left the restaurant even ten seconds later, we would not have witnessed this. Such is the perfection of the Universe.

I'm not one to follow many rituals; however, one of the best habits I have ever developed is that I express gratitude for what I love and appreciate in my life, before I get out of bed every morning. Even if I need to get up prematurely for whatever reason, I'll return to bed, settle back into my quiet space, and show gratitude to God, even if for just a moment. This is a great way to begin the day.

My awareness of angelic presence is especially strong right after I wake up and just before I fall asleep; both are very powerful times for expressing gratitude and setting intentions. By the way, at night, just prior to falling asleep, is an excellent time to speak of a problem; then you can let it go and allow your creative intelligence to take over while you sleep.

When you are experiencing difficulty after difficulty, can you bless these problems and even feel gratitude for them? Can you forgive those who created the difficulties? When we choose to forgive, can we also choose to be grateful for whatever gift came out of the wrongdoing? When we do this, we can achieve a greater sense of closure following the wrongdoing and gain wisdom from it, all with the miracle-producing effects of gratitude.

Those souls who have the greatest and most numerous challenges are also the ones moving toward significant growth in this lifetime. They are mastering major life lessons and passing the tests necessary for spiritual advancement. So, if you feel you have truly gone through the wringer, if you've been bombarded again and again with difficulties coming from all directions, know and appreciate the spiritual gain that will result. "Well," some of you may say, "I don't want to grow so much; I want life to be easier." That's probably not what you said prior to your arrival on this planet.

When we choose to seek the good in the bad, we master life. The good is always there, although looking for it can sometimes feel excruciating—that is the test. Miracles and love can find their way into any situation. Look at the 9/11 tragedy. People all over the world showed compassion and offered prayers for all those affected. It brought out the worst but also the best of humanity.

A telling example of this is the fact that years after the unimaginable occurred, there are "hundreds of thousands of people who have pledged to memorialize those killed on 9/11 by doing something good for others" ("In 9/11 remembrance, a turning to good deeds," *YAHOO! News*, September 11, 2007). A brother and a friend of a fallen 9/11 hero founded www.myGoodDeed.org, and by the sixth anniversary of 9/11, more than a quarter of a million people had pledged good deeds.

Speaking of good deeds, just prior to sending this book into production I felt guided to turn on the news. About ten seconds into the broadcast, I was delighted to hear a story about a lady at a Washington Starbucks' drive-through who paid for the stranger behind her, which set off an incredible chain reaction of more than eight hundred customers treating the "next in line." The lady who started the generous act tried doing this before but it never caught on. With some prodding from the barista, this time it worked. (CNN, December 22, 2007). New ways of thinking and being really can create a better world. This very positive news report will undoubtedly and exponentially set off a chain reaction of many more random acts of kindness.

You may feel like the eternal optimist, always looking for the good in everything. But is that a bad thing? That doesn't mean we ignore the hurt and pain of difficult things, especially the insurmountable grief of 9/11, but we can seek the good within the gloom and despair. We take something awful and turn it into something good. The good can always be found if we allow ourselves to look and be open—and that includes being open to miracles.

Miracles bless our lives when we practice our ultimate goal, demonstrating unconditional love and forgiveness. Everyone we know, including strangers, are constantly giving us opportunities to engage in these highest states of being. Synchronicity often reminds us of our need to love and forgive unconditionally, above all else, and shows us the way.

Several years ago, I experienced one of the worst nights of my life because of a phone call; what transpired hurt me deeply and shook me to the core. Shortly afterward, on this late night, I was driving in my subdivision, and a song came on the radio. Just as Don Henley sang the words, "It's about forgiveness ... forgiveness," from the song "The Heart of the Matter," a German shepherd darted in front of my car, and I slammed on the brakes. The meaning of the sign was crystal clear. I didn't hit the dog, by the way. And yes, my car does seem to attract dogs, but they are always okay.

Before I had the chance to even process my swelling pain and anger, I was being asked to forgive. The person I'd argued with over the phone was someone I truly loved, and I needed to feel that love and connect with those feelings, even though I was broken, my heart felt shattered, and I'd barely recognized the person on the phone that evening. I realized that my love was still there and that it truly was unconditional. If I couldn't forgive right away, I needed to move toward forgiveness. That was my lesson. I was convinced that this lesson was monumental and that it was absolutely vital for my growth. I was being called to rise above a most hurtful situation and decide right then and there to forgive.

I couldn't get over how premature it seemed to forgive before I could even swallow what had occurred, yet the wiser part of me realized that I would need to progress to a place where forgiveness would come this easily and immediately. *I was convinced that I needed to learn to reside in the state of unconditional love and forgiveness, no matter what was going on outside of myself.*

Had someone told me that I needed to forgive immediately, the message would not have been nearly as powerful. I would have thought, "Yeah, yeah, that's the right thing to do, but I'm too mad to do anything about it." However, when the Universe shows you, it shakes you into understanding. There was absolutely no denying the message.

I have no doubt that I was guided into the car late on that December night so that both the perfect lyric and the dog, in one powerful moment, would present an undeniable sign that I could not possibly miss. I retain that unforgettable memory as a symbolic reminder to always move toward love and forgiveness without condition.

Sometimes it's too difficult or even impossible to forgive someone in person. If the friend, acquaintance, stranger, or family member you wish to forgive is too hard to be with in the same space, is dangerous to be around, or is no longer living, there is another way to forgive. With intention, you can just feel and speak the words of forgiveness to this person's spirit: "I fully forgive _____." What you are doing is putting a halt to your own pain and setting *yourself* free. You are also breaking the negative energetic ties between you, which are unhealthy for both your spirits.

Often, it is ourselves that we need to forgive. Perhaps we're not even aware of our self-anger, but it is vital to direct the same unconditional love and forgiveness to ourselves, even before forgiving others. Take care of yourself first. You can release the same negative energy that is held within by feeling and speaking words of love and forgiveness to the self.

Forgiveness sometimes takes time to accomplish. But as we grow spiritually, we find that we don't have to be right about everything and can just let some things go, no matter how unfair. This is a difficult lesson for me, one that I'm still working to master. When I am misunderstood or treated unfairly or when someone neglects to take responsibility for their harmful actions, I just get undone.

The fact is, we just aren't always fully heard, and, even if we are, people misperceive each other, whether by conscious choice or not, all the time. It is also true that we can project our own problems onto each other, and so often how we judge each other is really a result of our own projections. Regardless, you get to a point where you've done all you can and you just throw up your arms and surrender to that situation that begs forgiveness. You realize that the grief and anger you hold within are only hurting you.

I often ask myself, in the big scheme of things, how much does this or that conflict really matter? We're all going to arrive in Heaven, and will we really care then anyway? It is all lesson. Things are going to occur, and we are going to get hurt sometimes. The grand lesson is all in our reactions to our negative experiences—to stand above it. When we master this, we don't have to suffer further by continually attracting more of it, with new faces and new situations.

When we love and forgive unconditionally and live in a state of gratitude, we are creating a more desirable and miraculous life. We also become examples for others. As we become more loving and appreciative, we naturally don't want to be around negative energies of anger and gossip. It becomes harder to listen to someone complain on end. When we truly master the ultimate lessons of unconditional love and forgiveness, we evolve. When love and forgiveness are felt on the individual level, these feelings translate eventually, after reaching critical mass, to love and forgiveness on a global level. The earth responds and evolves with us.

CHAPTER 15

THE ANGELS AMONG US

I frequently suggest to friends and clients that they ask their angels for help with their difficulties, as well as manifesting their desires. Angels are with us all the time, and we are never alone. They are our helpers, our listeners, our runners, and our friends. However, they cannot interfere, because we have free will. We need to simply ask them for assistance.

Imagine what it would be like to have a best friend who loves you, maybe even more than you love yourself. Always right at your side, this friend offers constant and unconditional love and support. When you seek success, this friend is your greatest cheerleader. If you act irresponsibly or in a hurtful manner, this friend still loves you even if you don't think you deserve to be loved. When you feel alone, this friend never leaves you. But what if you have this ideal friend without even knowing it? And, because you aren't aware, you don't acknowledge or feel gratitude for what this friend constantly does for you?

That's the way it is for most of us. We go through life unaware that our angels are loving us, watching over us, and celebrating us all the time. Their greatest desire is to serve us. But we must ask. We *must* ask! They deeply want us to. I can't fathom a more frustrating job than that of a guardian angel, although, I imagine that residing in blissful Heaven must help them to cope with the frustrations of our blindness. Yet times are changing, and we are becoming more and more enlightened about what is going on in the unseen realities.

Our angels send us incredible signs all the time. When I realized at one point that I was neglecting the practice of asking my angels for help, one experience got me back on track. I was feeling quite frustrated over whether I should pursue a particular project. A weight was lifted when I realized the needlessness of shouldering so much angst over the decision. As I was driving out of the subdivision to take my kids to school, I asked the angels to show me a sign that would reveal whether I should pursue this opportunity.

After driving a mile down the road, a policeman stopped me. "Was I speeding?" I wondered. I felt upset and embarrassed to have this happen in front of my kids. The policeman approached the car and asked me for my driver's license. He took the card into his hand, looked me in the eyes, and said, "Just slow down, Mary. I'm not going to give you a ticket; just slow down." He was the kindest police officer I'd ever encountered. Thank you, angels. I got your message loud and clear: to "just slow down, Mary." I chose not to pursue the project and felt confident that it was the right decision.

Why is it so difficult to just ask? Why is it so hard to even remember to ask? Is it partly because we don't feel worthy of angelic help? But we *are* deeply worthy; it is our Divine birthright to work with the angels. We're spiritual beings, just like they are. We have donned physical bodies and from birth are made to forget who we really are—that is, until we allow ourselves to remember.

You can choose to make it a habit to ask your angels for help. When practiced, this action can change your life on a dime. I'm sometimes asked how one is supposed to request their angels' help. I ask right back, "How do you ask a friend for help?" Speak to them as you do to your friend. You can do so in your mind or out loud.

Because we are indeed spiritual beings, should we not learn to feel and act like spiritual beings and be who we really are? When you let go of the fear of the unknown and open yourself up to new expressions from the Heavenly realms, they will naturally occur in your life. Have you ever felt tingling sensations on the crown of your head, as if there were a puddle of extremely effervescent soda water there? More and more people are feeling unusual sensations as the veil keeps thinning and humans become more open to these types of experiences.

Many believe that these sensations come from God, their angels, or their departed loved ones. Some people feel actual sensations on their skin at various places on their bodies. Others notice their arms or faces being gently moved or feel as if someone is brushing a finger through their hair. When you open yourself to these experiences, you feel blessed by the spiritual connection.

My greatest spiritual blessing is my conscious relationship with a particular archangel. In July of 2001, I became aware that an angel was communicating with me. His name was Thomas, and I channeled that he was preparing me for communication with Archangel Michael. Surely this was in my imagination, a statement I made in my mind countless times in the succeeding months. However, in November of that year, I began to receive information from Archangel Michael. I channeled many messages over the next several weeks through clairsentience, a psychic sensing or knowing, which is an ability we are all born with. It's as if you're hearing words, but it is through a knowingness and without sounds.

Please note that where I write things such as "I heard Michael say" or "Michael told me," I refer not to a sound but to a knowingness—a type of hearing that does not involve my ears. I'm not normally a clairaudient (one who psychically hears) or a clairvoyant (one who psychically sees). In the beginning, I questioned and doubted much of the information I was receiving.

One evening, while taking a long drive from Las Cruces to Albuquerque in late December, I channeled Michael the whole way home. At one point, he said he had a name for me. In my mind, I "saw" the letters S-O-L-I-E-L. I asked out loud, "So-leel?" "No," I heard him say, and then I knew that it was phonetically pronounced "Sol-ee-ehl." Was this really happening? I thought it was my mind playing tricks on me.

Michael told me to find the numerology of both his and my name on the numerology chart when I returned home, which I did. I found that Archangel Michael's name was a 12. To my surprise and delight, Mary Soliel was also a 12. That was the beginning of 12:12 synchronicities to occur in connection with Michael. By the way, I'm writing this chapter on 12/12/06, in his honor, but that isn't a surprise, is it?

In the spring of 2002, my kids and I visited a park near Las Cruces for an overnight stay so we could do some serious rock hounding, an ideal family outing for us nature lovers. As I'm writing this, I recognize the commonality that I've been to the Las Cruces area only twice, and both times were very relevant in affirming my connection to Michael. The day before we had left on the trip, Michael asked me to be aware of a sign from him among the rocks. When we were a couple of hours into our treasure searches, I was frustrated that I couldn't find the sign. I was on a constant lookout for it, yet nothing appeared meaningful. However, the sign would actually find me, as it turned out, and through none other than my children.

My son found a rock and excitedly said, "Mom! Look at this!" Scott placed into my hand a unique and beautiful piece of volcanic rock. I was speechless when I immediately realized it looked just like a flower; each of the five petals and the center were bubbled (see photo). Michael said in several channels that I'm "a flower about to bloom."

Just a couple of seconds after Scott handed the rock to me, Karen, who was rarely curious about the time, especially when engrossed in an activity such as this, asked, "What time is it, Mom?" I looked at my watch. "It's 12:12!" I exclaimed with pure joy. Leave it to my beautiful kids to present my sign so perfectly; there was no need for me to frantically search for a sign that would actually find me at the most perfect moment in time. I then realized that I needed to trust in my ability to channel, but the truth is that I continued to question things I heard for several more months.

Until writing this book, I have shared my connection to Michael with very few. One of them was my friend Kat, who was very familiar and comfortable with the idea of channeling. When I told her that Michael calls me "Soliel," she asked if I realized that *sol* means "sun" in Spanish. I knew that but for some reason I never really put it together. (I later learned that *sol* means "sun" in several other languages as well.)

He is calling me "angel of the sun" then, I said, because *iel* is the ending of many angels' names (such as Ariel, Gabriel, and Uriel). Why it took more than six months to come to that realization I don't know, but I think it was because it sounded so grandiose, and I don't feel any more special than the next person. But the fact is, we are *all* grandiose! We all are beautiful spiritual beings, so powerful beyond measure. Most of us are unaware of our magnificence and the fact that we each have access to our higher selves, our angels and archangels, and the Heavenly realms. And every one of us has the ability to channel, as well, if we so desire.

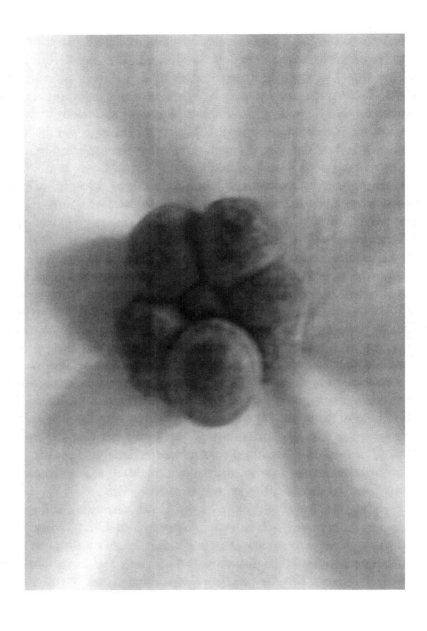

One week after I accepted this new understanding of my name, my family left for a trip to Maui, in the summer of 2002. Just before we left, Michael told me that I would see a ring in Hawaii that I must have and wear, as a symbol of our bond.

Just as with the rock, I was looking too hard for the ring. I spent hours going into nearly every jewelry shop in Lahaina, with no luck. I just wanted a simple silver band with a simple symbol of a sun but couldn't find anything I liked or that was my style. When was I going to learn? I finally realized I needed to patiently allow Michael to "present" it to me in his own way, even though I was so excited to find the symbol. As it turned out, my connection to Michael was even more significant than I had allowed myself to believe.

About halfway through the trip, I felt a strange urge to go down to the hotel gift shop during a lazy afternoon. I dislike touristy items and am not a shopper by any means unless I'm shopping for books, but I followed the feeling and told my family I was going to take a quick look there. My life would never be the same after that visit. What would occur was the most profound synchronicity I have ever experienced—beyond my wildest imagination.

I walked around the store, clueless as to why I was there. The store did not sell any rings, so it wasn't for that reason. I later realized that I channeled my need to be there, that Michael had surely whispered it to me. I eventually walked over to the handful of books on display, a collection of only seven different publications.

One immediately caught my eye. It was about the prophet Nostradamus, called *Prophecies for America*, but it was a new interpretation of his predictions, so it grabbed my attention. I thought it was incredibly strange that there would be a book about Nostradamus, one of just a handful of books being sold in a luxury hotel in Maui. I wondered how many people would actually desire reading about catastrophic prophecies while sunbathing in paradise. And how many hotels in the whole world were displaying it? Just one? But the Universe made sure I saw this book while visiting the "Island of the Sun."

Holding the book in my hands, I opened it to a certain page. My eyes went directly to a paragraph that referred to the archangels who were said to rule specific periods of time in history. It said, "We are living under the rulership of Michael, the angel of the Sun." *Michael! The angel of the Sun!*

I closed the book and went wide-eyed, feeling as if I'd gone out of my body. How could this be happening to me, a little speck of a being on this planet? Then I heard Michael tell me to move a few feet over. It was a knowingness to just move where he wanted me to be, and so I did. He then wanted me to open the book again, to that very page. I found it immediately, and a drop of water fell right onto that paragraph, covering those very words.

Above me, I saw some condensation at the edge of a ceiling air vent; I had been moved so that I'd be standing at the right spot and the drop would fall on the right place, reinforcing the message in case I somehow tried to explain it away. The fact was, I could never question my connection to Michael again. I could never question the connections we all have to the angels and archangels. The veil between Heaven and earth thinned to nearly nothing during this most astounding moment of my life.

As if that weren't enough, when I went to purchase the book, the clerk who sold it to me had the name "MaryChris" displayed on her name badge. To me, this symbolized my recognizing the Divine ("Christ") part of me. From the time Michael gave me my new name, he was mirroring Divine connection in miraculous ways. It was then and there that I needed to release the illusion of my separateness from the Divine—the same illusion that needs to be released from *all* of us.

Synchronicity is what is perfect in this world. How impeccable was it that Kat, just a week before this miracle, helped me see past my insecurities so I could embrace the true meaning of my name? Then, this meaning was perfectly validated by a miraculous chain of events that resulted in my ultimate transformation.

In my dozens of trips to many different bookstores over the years since this book about Nostradamus was published in October, 2001, I never saw that book, before or since that day in the hotel gift shop, except in its now prominent place in my personal library. But there it was at the perfect time and the perfect place, amazingly situated among a tiny display of just six other books.

The evening before we left Maui, my family and I went to a mall to pick up dinner at a food court. I kept feeling drawn to it when driving by, even though I'm not at all a fan of shopping malls. As we entered the building, we walked right next to a jewelry stand. There it was. The ring was just what I'd envisioned, a simple sterling silver band with a simple figure of the sun—perfect. The ring found me! In what seemed to take about two minutes, I spotted, tried on, and bought the ring, just like that. No wonder I'd felt so driven to visit that mall (thank you for the whispers, dear Michael). I have been wearing my ring from Michael every day since, with thoughts of our connection every time I put it on.

Two years after this life-altering trip to Maui, I divorced my husband. In the few months preceding it, I considered legally changing my name to "Mary Soliel" but with much anguish. My intense fear of what others would think of me if I changed my last name to something totally unexpected was clouding my objectivity. I chose to confide in my healer about my connection with Michael and the related synchronicities. I had already made an appointment to see her, and I would ask her to help me see clearly regarding this issue.

Prior to my appointment on a typically sunny day in New Mexico, I was driving my kids to school. Just the night before, I'd told my son about my relationship with Archangel Michael for the first time. If I was going to change my name, I needed to first share my connection to Michael with my kids, so I first told Scott.

As I held thoughts and concerns in my mind about changing my name, I turned the corner, looked up into the sky, and gasped out loud at what I saw. My daughter, who knew nothing about the "angel of the sun" synchronicity yet, said, "Look at the sun, Mom! There are angel wings around it!" I looked at my son, and he was as wide-eyed as I was, having just learned of my relationship with Michael the night before. There were two clouds in the form of perfect angel wings on each side of the sun, and I had my question answered. I didn't need to go outside of myself and search for an answer. *Gulp.* The worries about what my parents, friends, or acquaintances would think about my new name paled in comparison to my newly found courage and realization that I was destined and guided to carry this name.

When meeting with my lawyer to discuss drawing up divorce papers, I asked her if I could legally change my last name at the time of the divorce. She affirmed that I could and added, "You can be anyone you choose; you could even be 'Mary Sunshine' if you want." I couldn't believe she'd said "Mary Sunshine," as this was even more validation, through my lawyer this time! I responded, "Well, actually I was thinking along those lines. I want to change it to 'Mary Soliel.'"

We discussed temporary alimony, as I had been a stay-at-home mom for twelve years. She said that if I became a best-selling author, I could just tell Jack, "Thanks, but I don't need your help anymore." She had no idea I had a book "in me." My hope is that she was just as prophetic with that comment as she'd been with her previous one.

If you're wondering whether I'm "all there," I assure you I am. When you open yourself to the angels and to the magic of synchronicity, you may have people wondering if you're "all there" as well, because the unimaginable will happen for you. I hope you already know exactly what I'm talking about.

The angels are showing us that we are never alone. For you who are single and feel so alone, or you who are married or with a significant other and still feel so alone; for the homeless, the parentless, the childless, the young and old—the fact is *not one* of you is alone, not even for a moment. We are all constantly in the excellent company of angels. We are all, each and every one of us, assigned to archangels as well. They hear and respond to us all the time, no matter how many millions are calling on them at any given moment.

Please listen very carefully, because right now your angels are fully aware that you are reading these words. From the moment I began writing this book, I feel the angels have been applauding the potential that you may now—if you haven't already—choose to connect with them. Those in the Heavenly realms knew exactly who would find themselves attracted to the message here. Synchronicity took care of that. They have been waiting for you to have this book in your hands and read these words, so that you, each and every one of you, can, if you don't yet, have a conscious relationship with them. Speak to them as if they are your friends, right now, and see what unfolds.

*   *   *   *

Whenever you connect to the spirit side, ask for guidance from only those beings that are of the light and who are in line with your highest interest. There can be no darkness where there is light. Your demand will allow those only of the light to guide you. Your sincere intentions make that so. You are that powerful.

CHAPTER 16

CONNECTING WITH THE
HEAVENLY REALMS

*I*n October of 2006, a friend of mine lost her beloved young adult son to suicide. One moment everything was fine, and the next Cyd's whole world fell completely apart. She e-mailed me often following the tragedy, as it was cathartic to write down her overwhelming grief-filled thoughts and feelings. On the morning of Josh's funeral, she expressed how she desperately wanted to know he was all right. Her daughter had sensed his spirit presence in the family home, but Cyd hadn't yet noticed any signs of him.

She specifically asked if I could try to get in touch with Josh. Although I have received messages from some family members and friends who have passed on, from time to time, I've never shared that with anyone and was surprised she'd asked. As it turned out, Cyd's request was Heaven-sent and most perfectly timed, but it wasn't me who would channel a message.

Remarkably, I received her e-mail just minutes prior to leaving my home for an all-day workshop for healing practitioners taught by a gifted healer and *medium* (one who channels those who have passed), now of all times, the very day of his funeral—the day when Cyd most desperately wanted to feel a connection with Josh.

Actually, the workshop had been scheduled for the month prior but was canceled at the last moment. When the workshop was rescheduled, I was disappointed because I was already committed to teaching a class and would be unable to attend the second day of it. After I explained the conflict, the teacher assured me that I could attend just the first day of it, which provided the majority of instruction, to which I then agreed. All the forces were working perfectly.

I chose not to tell Cyd about the workshop. Why get her hopes up that this medium would take a special request for a reading? But I also felt this was too synchronistic to not work out. Early on during the class, I told the medium what had happened to my friend and that she was desperately reaching out for connection. The medium acknowledged that Josh's spirit was indeed with us but that she wasn't "open" at the time, being in a teaching mind-set. She said that if she became "open," she would channel a message.

At the last possible moment of the class, the medium poured forth a message that expressed that Josh was fine, why he'd ended his life, and that he loved his mother. He communicated a desire to connect with Cyd and said he would contact her in what the medium thought to be a few weeks of earth time, as there is no time in the spirit world. The medium explained that Josh was having difficulty transitioning and communicating at the time. But one night, his mother's phone would ring, and no one would answer. That would be her cue to lie down in bed and say, "Okay, I'm listening."

As soon as I returned home that night, I wrote Cyd about what had happened. In this woman's darkest hour, she was also blessed with the message that her son was okay and wanted to reconnect. I assured her that I had not shared any details about Josh with the psychic. As I learned from Cyd's reply later that night, most everything in the message resonated with her.

However, the medium indicated that Josh was an Indigo and had a hard time dealing with his gifts—hearing voices and so on. Cyd, like most people, had never heard of the term *Indigo*, as it isn't yet mainstream information. I explained that they are the new kids who are carrying the new energy and that they are here to help bring peace to the world. They are often labeled with ADD or ADHD. You know them by their special gifts and by their eyes. Because they are different, they don't easily fit in with others.

Cyd was shocked, because her son had been diagnosed with ADD as a child. Also, just days before the funeral, her daughter had said that although he was very likable, he somehow just didn't fit in. When they were sorting through pictures just after Cyd found out about Indigos, they found one that blew Cyd away. She had seen it a million times before, she explained, but not like then. The photo had been taken at his first birthday party. "The look in his beautiful eyes … I can't describe it," she wrote me. "And if you saw it, you would get it. Indigo."

As it turned out, Cyd never did get that call in the night. Spiritualist and author Mark Macy says that he receives calls from the spirit world. In an interview ("Breaking Through: Spiritualists say they communicate with the dead," *Boulder Daily Camera*, December 30, 2006), he states, "The caller ID says 'out of area,' which is kind of an understatement, I guess." So although there are some of us, myself included, who believe that this phenomenon occurs, for some reason, she didn't experience it. However, the medium's prophecy ended up enlightening someone else.

When I told my friend Julie about Cyd's tragic loss and the miracle of that reading just when she needed it most, I also mentioned the medium's advice to listen for the phone call with no one on the other end. Julie said that was so funny, because last night and this morning she got a call, and when she went to pick up the phone, no one was there. I told her that I strongly felt it was her father, who died several years ago. She wasn't very believing. I asked her if there was something special about this day, and she said, "It's his birthday today." A smile spread across my face. No doubt her father's spirit planned this, knowing what I knew, knowing I'd be compelled to tell his daughter about it—all synchronistic and so perfectly planned.

Eventually, Cyd received several signs from Josh. The first one occurred when she was in her kitchen making dinner while talking to her husband. She suddenly stopped what she was doing, aware of a familiar scent. It was Josh's smell. She told her husband she could smell Josh, and when he walked to where she was standing, he agreed that it was definitely him.

The most powerful sign from Josh came in a most unexpected way, nearly seven months after he passed. Cyd was introduced online to a fellow mother who'd also lost her son, Brian, to suicide. They exchanged e-mails for a while, and then, at one point, this woman told Cyd that a well-known medium was going to perform a psychic reading of her son and told her the date it would occur.

On the day before the reading, Cyd started asking Josh to find Brian, this other young man who'd passed on. "Josh, go find Brian," she said in her mind and out loud. And then she would say, "Brian, you don't know me, but go find Josh." Or she would say, "Brian, go find my Josh, and let him know that I need to hear from him." She repeated these words again and again—when in the shower, at work, when driving—many times throughout the day, because she'd made the conscious choice to speak these words instead of crying when she felt sad.

The following day, which was when the reading was to occur, Cyd opened a package, which she expected to contain a book about Indigo children. When she had told her former boss about that medium's comment that Josh was an Indigo, he later told his hairdresser about it. The hairdresser said that she'd just ordered a book about Indigo children and that even though she hadn't read it yet, she wanted Cyd to have it. It actually took months for Cyd to receive it. She tried to arrange to pick it up but, strangely, wasn't able to do so on many occasions. The timing was never right, as if the pickup was being delayed until the day that would synchronistically make the most impact. She was finally able to pick it up on that perfect day, the morning of the reading. But the book was not about Indigos, as she'd been told.

Rather, Cyd was surprised to find a book titled *Matthew, Tell Me About Heaven: A Firsthand Description of the Afterlife*. Written by a bereaved mother, it contains telepathic conversations between her and her passed son. As Cyd explained it to me, "There was that first nudge at synchronicity, a book about a mother and her son communicating after he passed." After looking at the book, she decided to check her e-mail, and waiting in her inbox was a message for her that took her breath away.

Brian's mother had sent an e-mail to several people, including Cyd, titled "My reading with Brian." She explained that the reading had not occurred, because another spirit had come through and would not leave. He had been very insistent, so Brian had let him through. This other spirit had repeatedly spoken to the medium the words, "Gunshot to the right of the head." Cyd was in shock; she knew immediately and without a doubt that this spirit had been Josh. Tragically, he'd killed himself in exactly this way, and he used the most raw and convincing words to prove to his mother that it was indeed him.

Cyd had made this happen; she'd called for these boys' spirits to meet. Josh had been so insistent and impassioned to make a connection with his mother that the reputable medium had been unable to continue the reading. The medium called it "brain block," which apparently can happen sometimes. Because Cyd never told Brian's mother how Josh had committed suicide, she had no idea what the medium was talking about—that is, until Cyd replied to her e-mail to tell her. She also explained that she'd called the two boys together.

So many forces had come together for this to happen: the online meeting between the two mothers and the person who'd brought them together to begin with; a mother's unstoppable determination to connect with her son by asking the boys to find each other; the unexpected book that came months later than expected but on the very day that would mirror what was just ahead; and the medium who would have the ability to clearly interpret Josh's emphatic message. The synchronicities behind this event resulted in a highly desired validation for Cyd.

In order to further connect with her son, Cyd set up her own reading with this medium. Much of the channeled information firmly validated that Josh's spirit was present. Yes, he had a younger sister, played drums, and drove a sporty car. When Cyd asked what she should do with his car, he said, "Send it to me!" Then he added, laughing, "Or dip it in bronze!" Josh had possessed a great sense of humor and had been very witty, and that obviously hadn't changed; this provided further evidence that Josh truly had made contact.

The medium said that Josh made several references to him being one of Cyd's guides now. She would be able to communicate with him directly, and he wanted to help her. What a testament this is to the love between this mother and son. Whether on earth or in Heaven, love endures. We never die; we just transition.

Cyd shared with me a website for those dealing with grief from the death of loved ones. It helped her to cope by communicating with others dealing with loss via an online message board, on which they also shared their experiences of communications and signs from their loved ones. I went to the site and saw her entry, along with several responses to her grief.

As I scrolled down to other entries, I saw a headline about triple numbers on the clock, which of course got my immediate attention. A woman, whose loved one had passed, wanted to know why she woke up every night at the same exact time; she wondered whether it was just a coincidence. I wrote her that I felt it was her passed loved one nudging her awake at the same remarkable time, to prove to her that this loved one was fine and was watching over her.

The act of visiting this site set off a chain reaction of several remarkable synchronicities connected with the message board, all within a very short span of time. Before I describe them, allow me to remind you that profound synchronistic meanings are often found in the smallest, seemingly insignificant details of everyday life.

When I joined my friend, Cynthia, for coffee, we began talking about the books each of us were writing. After a while, I suggested we take a walk, and I playfully alluded to the idea that we could attract some coins on the sidewalk. I was referring to something in T. Harv Eker's book, *Secrets of the Millionaire Mind*, which we'd both read. From this book, I learned that one of the ways we can attract wealth is to always pick up coins seen on the ground, to get excited about receiving money even if it's a penny, and to show gratitude to the Universe for it.

So we set off on our walk while talking about our projects. I began to say to Cynthia that I needed to trust that my book would unfold perfectly. The moment I said "trust," I looked down to find three pennies aligned right in front of my next step. We marveled at the timing and that there were three pennies. This was a beautiful validation for me.

Later that day, I went online to the website for those in grief only to find an entry on the message board about how coins are used for after-death communications (ADC). ADCs are various types of communications and signs from deceased loved ones and friends. It went on to explain how the date on the coins can carry significance, such as the year the loved one was born or any connection relative to the year, something I'd never thought of.

The following day, while I was teaching a class on becoming a conscious creator, one of my students noted, without my having brought up these stories, that she'd woken up three times the night before. Each time on the clock represented the date of birth of her, her husband, and her son. It gave her a sense that all was well with all three of them.

The day after that, I woke and noticed that my clock had stopped with both hands on the number 2. That morning, I went to the website and saw an entry about a woman's clock stopping. The entry described this woman's belief that this event was not an ADC from her loved one but rather a normal occurrence caused by a malfunctioning clock.

It had been years since a clock or watch of mine just stopped, and I wrote this woman that it was no coincidence that my experience had occurred just prior to reading her entry. I felt it was absolute confirmation for her that she had received an ADC from her passed loved one. This is another perfect example of how we truly are messengers for each other.

This unusual string of synchronicities in my own life, which were connected to messages on the website occurred, I believe, so that I could act as a messenger for those on the message board as well as for you, the reader—particularly for those of you who are grieving the loss of a loved one. Your loved ones can indeed communicate with you and you need only be open and aware.

Regarding the coin phenomena, I recently took some time to walk up and down Pearl Street, the popular outdoor mall in Boulder, just to get exercise, as we are still recovering from a couple of winter storms. I kept my head down, looking for coins, nearly the whole time. I didn't even see a penny. When I was several blocks from my car, the odd thought crossed my mind that it would be so funny if, at the last possible step before I reached my car, I found a coin. I admit that it was a strange thought, but I truly did think that. As I approached my car, I saw on the pavement, right next to the driver-side door, a shiny quarter in a small puddle of clear water.

I believe that my thought was clearly heard by the angels, and thus I manifested that coin exactly where I'd imagined it. It was a very magical moment. I felt like Charlie when he found the golden ticket in the movie *Willy Wonka and the Chocolate Factory*. I realize how this may sound to you. However, this really happened, and the same kind of thing is happening to many others. People are seeing pennies, feathers, and even rubber bands suddenly appearing in places where there was nothing only moments before. Among these people are those who consider the appearance of these items to be attempts by their departed loved ones to connect with them.

When my friend Connie saw a penny on the ground, she picked it up and said to the coin, "You are a thousand dollars!" She was on her way to see her parents. Upon her arrival, her father told her that he was very proud of her and wanted her to have something. It was a check for $1,000. Connie knows the secrets to manifestation. When she spoke to that coin, she knew it was already a done deal. She told me this story when I called her, "ironically" just after it happened. And what song was playing on her car radio when I phoned her? "Money" by Pink Floyd.

We are being blessed by those in the Heavenly realms all the time, even when we are in the depths of grief. When Cyd wrote me a particularly distressing e-mail one night, about her extreme difficulties in coping with her loss, I felt deeply saddened. Just as I finished reading the e-mail, my daughter exclaimed, "Josh!" and my son questioned, "Josh?" They were talking about a character on a television show, but, as you will recall, Josh was also the name of Cyd's son. At that moment, I heard something in my office, some kind of electrical sound, as if a light bulb had gone out, but very loud.

From experience, I know that spirits can affect electrical things in order to get our attention. Considering the fact that I'd read the e-mail, my kids had said his name, and the electrical sound had occurred all at the same time, I knew without a doubt that Josh was there with me. He asked me (I didn't hear his voice but had a knowingness) to tell his mother about "the feet washing."

Kryon, the channeled entity through Lee Carroll, often includes in his channeled messages that our feet are being "washed." It is an energetic washing and a beautiful expression of love from Kryon, and the angelic entourage also present, for those who congregate for the channels or later read them (these channelings are published through the enlightening Kryon book series).

Before ever hearing about the feet washing, I used to feel sensations on my skin and knew I was being touched by the Heavenly realms, so the idea of the "feet washing" didn't feel so foreign to me. I experienced it not just during these beautiful meetings, which I've attended many times, but also in my own space, usually at night when in my bed, and often when going through a challenging time. I also sometimes wake with these sensations, and it is a beautiful feeling and a blessed way to begin my day.

Until this point, I had not readily shared these experiences with others, but I needed to find the courage to write Cyd about it, even if she thought I was off my rocker. I was convinced that her son wanted to show his love for her in this way and to prove that he was every bit alive, just in another dimension. Some self-induced fears seeped in. What if nothing happened? What if she didn't feel it? It could end up causing her even more pain! However, I knew I had to release these thoughts and just trust, so I wrote her about it. Several days later, I called Cyd to check on her, and we talked for a very long time. I couldn't hang up, because I knew there was something I needed to say, and then it occurred to me.

"Have you experienced the feet washing by Josh?" As soon as I asked her, she said she felt this tingling all over her feet and lower legs. She said that until that moment, she hadn't felt it. Then Cyd said, "It's getting very intense now," so I told her I would hang up to let her be with it. She felt her son's presence and has since on several occasions. If you have any question as to whether you really do have angels or passed loved ones around you, ask them for a touch, for a feet washing, or for any sign as a way for them to show their presence and express love. Once you experience one of these sensations, you won't feel alone again. You will also be at peace, knowing that your loved ones who have passed truly are fine.

When I receive a message from the Heavenly realms that I find hard to believe or accept, I ask for confirmation with some kind of physical sensation. For instance, I'll say, "Show me by touching my left hand if I'm understanding this correctly." In my mind, I firmly direct this request to only those of the light. And sure enough, the tingling sensations in that area will confirm it. This type of validation is yours for the asking. Your relationships with your angels, as well as your passed loved ones, can be highly creative ones, with endless possibilities.

For the last twelve years, I have heard a sound that feels as if it's radiating in my head, not in my ears. It is not tinnitus. This sound is somewhat high-pitched, almost a soft whistle, but not irritating and rather comforting. It is always the same sound and only varies in intensity. I hear it every day and welcome it, because I know it is the sound of God. I feel I'm tuning in to all that is. Especially when reading something spiritual, having a deep conversation, or meditating, I hear this sound.

When there is something I need to know or pay attention to, I hear it and know that I'm tuned in. I've heard it constantly throughout the writing of this book. After all these years, I am so used to it that it has become part of me. I have read that many others experience the same thing, but as with other phenomena regarding our connections to the Heavenly realms, not much information has entered the mainstream yet.

At a time when I was experiencing much joy in my life, I sat in a comfortable chair and listened to music that touched me on a spiritual level. All of a sudden, I slipped into a blissful state, truly ecstatic, where I felt my whole body experiencing what felt like an intense orgasm. The sensations rolled throughout my being and lasted quite a while, and I, of course, did not want them to stop.

When I was a young girl, and well before I knew what an orgasm was, I had this knowingness, perhaps from memories of inter-life, that when angels and spirits meet, they feel really good, better than people could ever feel when on earth. Without knowing what an orgasm or the sexual act felt like, I recalled the ecstasy that is felt in Heaven, which I eventually came to believe is similar to an orgasm but much more intense.

Within those brief moments of orgasm that we experience here on earth is, I believe, a small taste of that energy, a form of that which is felt in Heaven. One's potentially negative beliefs regarding sex, especially that which is bred by the mass media's devaluing and desecration of most everything regarding it, can make this concept difficult and uncomfortable to accept. At this level, certainly in American culture, sex is hardly considered the sacred act it is designed to be. However, as the veils are thinning between Heaven and earth, as we are creating Heaven on earth, the experience of this sacred level of ecstasy is becoming increasingly commonplace and understood.

As I prepared for the final editing of this book, I made an etheric connection to my twin flame. Closer than our closest soul mate, the twin flame is the other half of our soul. Each and every one of us has a twin flame, and the relationship is a most intimate one, balancing both masculine and feminine energies. Never have I truly felt Heaven as a human being, on a day-to-day basis, as I have through this most loving experience of connection that is just beginning to unfold.

My understanding is that this is occurring with many others during these transformative times as we bring more love into the world. In our past incarnations, twin flames were usually (not always) separated, with one on earth and one in Heaven at any given time. I believe that during this present evolutionary time in history, this situation is different. I wonder if this is precipitating an actual union in the physical realm. Could it be that this is what was promised to me in that letter I received nearly twenty years ago, that a perfect relationship in human form, that emphasizes my relationship with Him, would be presented to me, as described in the chapter "Expect the Unexpected"?

The idea of hearing a spiritual sound, getting a feet washing from an angel, or feeling Heavenly ecstasy may sound so strange, maybe even frightening, but this may be only because the concept is new to us. As we open ourselves to the possibilities, we become more comfortable with our connections to the Heavenly realms. For most of us, the sudden appearance of an angel may give us a fright. Therefore, angels will show their presence in whatever way we can handle: whether they nudge us to look at the clock at a significant time or appear in their beautiful magnificence, right in front of our eyes.

I believe that our experiences have everything to do with intention. If we intend to have these experiences and don't fear them, we will experience them, and they will enrich our life experiences as human beings. An active, conscious relationship with an angel can be a highly creative act. Many of us are pioneers in forming these types of relationships, and we are finding that there is endless potential in our exchanges between Heaven and earth.

CHAPTER 17

ANYTHING IS POSSIBLE

*R*ichard Bach wrote in his book *Illusions*, "Argue for your limitations, and sure enough, they're yours." As synchronicities move through life with your focused awareness, the miraculous occurs and you set aside self-doubts, get out of the box of linear thinking, and see that anything is indeed possible. This is what miracles do for us. They open our hearts and minds to the infinite possibilities available to each of us.

My best personal example is the writing of this book. Since I was a teen-ager, I wanted to author a book. It seemed part of my destiny, but it also felt like such a pipe dream. I didn't think enough of myself then and doubted that people would actually be interested in what I had to say. I strongly argued for my limitations when I became a young woman, and owned them, for the most part, all these years until I made the firm deci-sion to write this book. It took the simple act of changing my mind. I real-ized that in a split second, anything can change. I proactively shifted from the self-created reality of pipe dreams to an "I can achieve anything I desire" paradigm.

My conscious spiritual path that began twelve years ago has now resulted in the surrendering of myself to the writing of this book. I know that when we follow our passion and purpose, everything lines up. It's like leaping off a cliff and knowing we will be supported. I've taken many leaps and don't regret any of them. With this book, I will be supported in all ways. I'm especially taking the leap of sharing my unusual adventures without allowing others' possible judgments of my once private thoughts and experiences to stop me from sharing my message.

As a side note, we are becoming much less private and more open as this world becomes increasingly connected. The Internet is a perfect example of this. Many are sharing personal thoughts and experiences on message boards and in chat rooms, especially the younger generation. We are more closely connected than ever before, not just because of our incredible ability to immediately access and share vast amounts of facts, thoughts, and material as we network, often socially, over the Internet but also through cell phones calls, text messaging, and e-mails; we are constantly in touch and exchanging information. And there seems to be a deeper reason for all of this.

Just as Heaven and our angels see all that is going on with us, we seem to be moving in that same direction with each other, through our advancing technologies. In a very strange way, technology seems to be helping to create this aspect of Heaven on earth, this feeling of exposure, connection, and oneness. However, on the negative end, this isn't always pleasant, because we are often subjected to overexposure as unwilling participants.

This morning, while at home, I was interrupted in my work when I received three phone calls within forty minutes, those irritating and disruptive recorded messages of solicitation. We normally receive them during dinner. Sadly, we don't have the same privacy we used to have—there is less respect and consideration for it. We are constantly bombarded with marketing messages, and even though we are all well aware of this fact, this bombardment is so constant that we are often numb to it (while our subconscious minds record everything, of course). In order to play a video news clip on the Internet, one is often forced to first watch an advertising message. Every seller needs to advertise to make buyers aware of their product's existence, but should buyers be manipulated into viewing a thirty-second ad just so they can view a short news clip, for example? Isn't this going a bit too far?

Wherever we go, our images are often captured on cameras. Many businesses know all about our buying habits. There are no secrets anymore. This is one leap we all seem to be taking—this strange leap into exposure and connectedness. And with this leap comes less privacy, with and without our consent.

But let's get back to your own personal leaps, the ones you do give consent to. They may challenge you in many ways. They may propel you into the spotlight. They may require you to trust that you'll have exactly what you need just in the nick of time and not a moment sooner. Regardless, when you take the leap into your greatest passion and purpose, expect miracles and think big. Make sure your brain doesn't confine you to a narrow view of your dream. Stay focused on your ultimate desire. Remove yourself from the box of limitations. Remember, you should think big!

When we follow our purpose, synchronicity allows for the necessary unfoldings as we maintain our awareness, courage, and determination. Additionally, the many talents we possess, the ones that are suppressed and lie dormant, will surface at the right time and often with the help of signs. We carry them with us from our past lives, and we may "grow them" in this life, if we so choose.

Those shining abilities, which we perhaps haven't yet embraced, will come forth easily and effortlessly when they are in line with our purpose. Their arrival represents a natural movement toward greatness in any area. Just as some people can pick up a guitar and immediately play it, or another can pick up a paintbrush for the first time and paint more brilliantly than someone who has spent a lifetime painting, these talents are already built in.

Of course, we don't have to be the greatest artists or musicians to succeed. Whatever our purpose is, it comes from an innermost desire, and the talents and abilities required to fulfill that desire will surface once they are called forth. When I led an after-school drawing club for my children's school, I knew that everyone there wanted to be there because it was not a required class but rather a club they chose to join. I began every meeting by having each child stand on a chair and pronounce out loud, "I am an artist," because they truly were artists—they had the desire and did the work. But I made sure they owned it, that they called it forth in order to achieve their own level of greatness. So I eventually had to learn to walk my talk.

I have always been nervous about speaking in front of groups and, as a result, always shied away from doing so. My mental chatter would go into high gear, and then I would worry about everything from what people thought of my physical appearance to how well I spoke. My anxieties would turn into a self-fulfilling prophecy, because I would become unnecessarily concerned and would inevitably fall short.

However, when I felt destined to teach spiritual development classes in recent years, I decided to confront my fear. I stood on a chair and said, "I am a teacher." I am just kidding. But I threw myself into it, and, to my surprise, I immediately felt like a natural at teaching. Although I was nervous for the first minute or so, a sense of peace then came over me. I articulated well throughout and enjoyed it tremendously. Students were surprised that it was my first class. I took a baby step, and it worked.

Making your big dreams come true requires varying levels of risk. Whether the risk involves standing in front of a class, using your hard-earned money to invest in your new purpose, or leaving a secure and well-paying job for something new that you feel more passionate about, you have to consider your risks. But as you adopt a more spiritual way of being, risks don't carry the same charge. You feel supported and naturally trust more, because you understand that the Universe is behind you. Thus, you are less prone to fear, which would only create the undesirable. The energy and time you save from not worrying and feeling fear can be spent much more effectively. When you're in line with your purpose, everything falls into place, and you can relax with the knowingness that you can make anything happen.

Often, people are your best messengers that anything is indeed possible. In the summer of 2006, I made a new friend, Cynthia. In a single conversation, we found out we had a tremendous number of things in common. We both grew up in Michigan. We both attended the University of Michigan. We both recently divorced and were single moms. We both were writing a book. We both were actively pursuing our spiritual paths. We both had healing and writing abilities. She had lived only a quarter mile away from where I'd just moved, and our street names had been the same. We are both Scorpios, and our birthdays are only four days apart. All this was revealed in one short exchange.

Through guidance from the Heavenly realms, I'm sure, we began to support each other with our book writing and shared the beginning pages of our manuscripts. We met on a couple of occasions to discuss our projects and encourage each other. I had a strong inner knowingness that her book's message was significant, even though my understanding of its contents was limited.

Something about our second meeting on December 10, 2006, propelled me to suddenly write furiously with a renewed and increased commitment to my project. That was the day when my book really began to write itself. Until then, I was stuck, hardly getting anywhere as the words did not flow. We later agreed that it was a magical day for both of us.

Two days later, I wrote the chapter about Archangel Michael. As soon as it was completed, I felt the strongest urge to send it to Cynthia, even though I'd promised I wouldn't keep sending her things, as she was so busy with her own writing. The feeling was so powerful that I e-mailed her the chapter without hesitation.

Cynthia e-mailed back with words of absolute amazement at how much we had in common, even with our books. In order to preserve her privacy, as I don't wish to prematurely unveil her own story, let me just say that there were connections that had us both stunned. And the Universe made sure we knew about them.

Talk about synchronicity bringing two people together for a common purpose and for many reasons. Cynthia lived in the south of France for several years. Just days after our exchange of information, it was channeled for me in a psychic reading that I had experienced lifetimes in the south of France and had been a healer there, so Cynthia's presence mirrored that awareness to me. This explained my yearning to travel to France for the last several years. It's so fascinating to me how synchronicity unveils the message, just at the time that will make the most impact, which then causes you to trust and embrace the information being illuminated.

We often feel connections to and pulls toward places we've lived before in previous lives. For many years, I've felt attracted to Machu Picchu in Peru. When I shared that a few years ago with Clare, my intuitive friend, she confirmed the connection for me. She told me that I had a past life there, and in ceremony, I would greet and worship the sun at every sunrise. Clare, who feels connected to the moon, honored the moonrise. A documentary recently broadcast about Machu Picchu portrayed the area as once being a place for solar worship (Machu Picchu, History Channel International, April 17, 2007). After watching with intense interest, I asked Clare if she knew that. She was

completely unaware, but, being an intuitive, she just had this knowingness
about our past lives there.

The synchronicity continued with such perfection that only the Universe could bring forth. After three months of daily visits to the same wonderful coffeehouse to write, I suddenly desired a change in environment, because it was always very busy and I was finding it increasingly difficult to find a table near an electrical outlet. On this day, when it was especially loud and cramped (as the forces probably made it seem so), I went to another local café just a mile away. This ended up becoming my new "office" away from my (home) office for a while.

On the second day there, I settled down at my new favorite table, which featured an adorable lamp shaped like the Eiffel Tower with a burgundy shade. I thought of Cynthia, because of her connection with France, and also of all the France synchronicities that had recently manifested in my awareness. When I attempted to plug my cord into the outlet just below my table, I saw that both outlets were being used, one for the lamp and the other by someone else. I looked behind me to see someone, whose back was to me, who was also using her laptop. So I just unplugged the lamp and was set to go. After working for a while, I got up to buy a cup of coffee, as the line had gotten much shorter, and when I came back to my table, I was flabbergasted to see who was sitting right behind me: Cynthia.

Certainly, our angels were laughing and celebrating when they saw our surprised faces. They no doubt had set this up. Did they whisper ideas or suggestions to us? Absolutely! This was the first time that Cynthia had come here to work, and it was only my second—even though we both lived close to this café. Plus, I was feeling a strong urge since yesterday (another whisper from the angels, I'm sure) to see if she could meet me for coffee, as it had been some time since we'd connected.

Both of us felt that our angels set this up so that we would further inspire each other to write. Having a friend to share your thoughts with, who is on a similar mission, can prove to be helpful. Neither of us had ever been involved in projects quite like this before. And we were guided to support each other as we tapped into our greatest potential in order to create our destined projects.

We are being asked to step into our magnificence like never before. We're seeing this more than ever, in all walks of life. Who would have thought, when Jennifer Hudson auditioned for *American Idol*, that a few years later she'd be accepting an Academy Award for Best Supporting Actress, for the whole world to see? She stepped into her magnificence in such a dramatic way that I still get goose pimples when I recall her performance in *Dreamgirls*.

Who would have thought that a man who'd found himself in a situation where he was unhappy, homeless, and hopeless would ask God a question that ultimately resulted in a long list of best-selling books? Neale Donald Walsch's *Conversations with God: an uncommon dialogue* marked the beginning of the conversation, resulting in a series of books that have enlightened millions of lives.

Did you hear about the stay-at-home mother who had the idea of placing little decorations in the holes on her kids' Crocs, those fun, colorful shoes, an idea that eventually made her a multimillionaire? When her seven-year-old daughter's decorated shoes were spotted by a man at the local pool, he asked her to give her mommy his business card and have her call him. This man happened to be the founder of Crocs! That so-called chance meeting—an example of synchronicity at its best—resulted in the selling of her "Jibbitz" business to Crocs for $20 million (as told on *The Oprah Winfrey Show*, ABC, February 2, 2007).

These are just a few examples that immediately come to mind among the endless stories out there. This is all about stepping into your passion, into your destiny, and then trusting—being aware of your path and walking it with courage and relentless determination. When you connect with your true purpose, great things happen.

This book practically wrote itself, and I believe it is just the beginning. I already have several new projects in the planning stages. When I have a moment of doubt about whether this book is going to be good enough, I just say, "If it isn't, *I will make it so.*" I don't have to know all the details right now; rather, I just *see* the finished product. I visualize myself holding the first printed copy of *I Can See Clearly Now* in my hands, and I feel ecstatic!

Throughout the writing of this book, I've made several trips to different bookstores, and each time, I imagine having book signings there. I go to the metaphysical section and see exactly where on the bookshelf my books will sit, since they are usually placed in alphabetical order by author. They'll be placed near the books of Margaret Starbird, who has written about Mary Magdalene; with all my synchronicities regarding Mary, that seems fitting.

There is already a space reserved in my home, clutter free, where I can house the books I will personally sell. I visualize holding each book in my hands before mailing it, throwing love and light on it and sending it with angels—my own prayer of gratitude that it fully benefits each receiver. The readers' angels are so excited, which makes me so excited.

Wow! Sarah McLachlan's song "Angel" started playing in the background at the café with the telling lyric "In the arms of an angel." It didn't come on a half hour ago or even minutes ago but rather just as I wrote about sending each book with angels. I share this, as it is most especially a blessing for you, reader.

For those of you who feel there is a book in you, and your heart is bursting to write it, just do it! Many new books need to be written. We are transitioning in unprecedented ways and need new information, new ideas, and new ways of thinking and being. If you feel passionate about getting your message out, just write and be relentless about it. "A professional writer is an amateur who didn't quit," said Richard Bach.

Whatever your unrealized dreams may be, think of author Anaïs Nin's famous saying, "And the day came when the risk to remain tight in a bud was more painful than the risk it took to blossom." What is your heart telling you? What is it aching for? Are you listening to your deepest desires? Will you take the leap? I hope that what I've shared with you in this chapter helps to inspire you to make an unrealized dream a reality and realize without a doubt that anything is indeed possible. Remember that the angels may work with others to support you and show you the way, so remain aware.

May you count on and fully expect synchronicity and your angels to help make your greatest dreams possible, and often just in the nick of time. This is called trust.

CHAPTER 18

WHAT'S WITH MOLLY AND THE ROSE?

*A*fter Cynthia and I had that synchronistic meeting at the coffee shop, where we sat back to back without our knowing, we decided to meet again in a couple of days. This time, we planned to watch the sunrise first and then write. There would be a solar eclipse on this day, and the spring equinox was to occur a couple of days later. Lately, I've been feeling a particularly strong urge to greet the sun's first appearance. I know it is a powerful practice to consciously connect with the energy of our brightest star and tune into nature's daily rhythms by recognizing sunrises, as well as sunsets.

On the morning of the eclipse, I woke to Seal's song "Kiss from a Rose" on my lips. Whenever I wake with a song on my mind, I listen closely, as it always carries meaning. I've experienced synchronicity with this beautifully mysterious song for years, ever since it came out in 1994, which happened to be the same year my conscious spiritual path began, but I hadn't been able to make a meaningful connection. Thirteen years later, I would reattempt to discover the significance. Earlier this particular week in March, there had been a surge in synchronicity with the song; something powerful was emerging.

The song played on my car radio just before I arrived for an appointment at my dentist's office. During the checkup, I heard the song play over and over in my mind. When I returned to the car, a happy childhood memory came into my awareness. I recalled, from out of the blue, when my grandma took me to see the stage musical *The Unsinkable Molly Brown.* I was a little girl at the time, and it was such a happy memory of just me with my beloved "Mary Mama," one of the closest people to my heart. She is in spirit now.

Why was the memory of this musical coming into my awareness? Nothing had occurred that would have triggered the recollection. The story was based on the famous Titanic survivor. Is it because, like Molly, I'm unsinkable? I do feel I am unsinkable; I feel like a Molly Brown. "Are you there, Mama?" I asked. With that question, I felt the presence of my grandma, and I just sat in the car taking it in. I am often aware of her watching over my children and me.

She is no doubt helping with the writing of this book and has supported me with my healing work as well. Her presence is felt subtly and quietly. However, I felt it strongest when she came to me in a dream when I was pregnant with my son. She told me that everything was going to be okay. It was so real that I woke up and cried so hard; my heart was re-breaking, feeling the loss of her again, fourteen years after her death. Now I've experienced thirty years of missing her in the physical, and in this moment sitting in the car, my connection with her spirit was especially profound.

Just when I was sure that my grandma had prompted me to recall the "Molly Brown" memory to show that she was with me, I soon found there was something more to her message. I had a vision of her floating above me and "sprinkling" snowflakes on my head. Immediately, I made the connection with the part of Seal's song when he sings about it snowing and how the light that is shown can be seen.

My grandma definitely had a message for me, and I needed to find the lyrics of "Kiss from a Rose" and put the pieces together, to somehow tie it in with the memory of Molly Brown. As much as I loved this song, I found its meaning vague. Of course, any one song can touch or give meaning in endless ways. It was important for me to discover my own personal connection with it, but up until now, the specific message wasn't clear. When I returned home on this eventful day, I went online to look up the lyrics. I then realized that all these years I had misunderstood and had been unaware of some of the words—and that's why the meaning had appeared vague.

As I'm writing this, a man in the coffee shop seated at the next table is talking about "lyrics of a song."

What first struck me was the sudden realization that the song begins by referring to what seems to be a lighthouse. My business name, when I lived in New Mexico, was called A Lighthouse in the Desert, LLC. After moving to Colorado, I changed it to A Lighthouse in the Rockies, LLC. I consider myself as one of the tens of thousands of "lightworkers" who incarnated on the earth at this time to shine the light, to be "lighthouses," through their work and everyday life.

As I pondered Seal's lyric "Now that your rose is in bloom," I realized that this echoed the message Archangel Michael had given me, that I'm a flower about to bloom. I then made the connection to all lightworkers. Are we "in bloom" and ready to really shine the light? Beyond that, Mary Magdalene is strongly identified with rose symbolism. What has "Kiss from a Rose" been saying to me all these years? Is it a way for me to recognize the call for lightworkers shining the light on the movement toward embracing the Divine feminine and all that Mary Magdalene symbolizes? Is this why I've always felt unexplainably drawn to her? This unfolding seemed complex and heavily destined, and I was determined to remain alert and open to the messages.

We all, men and women, have both male and female energies within us, and we are coming into a whole new balance of these energies. Those lower vibrations of the extreme male aspects of us (in both men and women), such as aggression and greed, are growing more unable to remain in the increasing presence of the predominant female aspects (in both men and women) of love, nurturing, compassion, and freedom. So, could it be that the lyric "rose is in bloom" is actually saying that the energy of the Divine feminine is now here?

When I woke up early this morning of the eclipse with the song running through my mind, I thought about the rose symbolism. I also recalled that Cynthia refers to Mary Magdalene in her book. I hoped that a greater understanding of this whole enigma would surface at the sunrise this morning.

As we waited for the show of light, I told Cynthia about my grand-mother and *The Unsinkable Molly Brown*, as well as the recent synchronic-ities with Seal's song. She said, "I can't believe you just said that!" In the book she is writing, her main character, named Rose, has a flashback to when she sang a song for a talent show. The song was from *The Unsinkable Molly Brown!* Even I, the synchronicity queen, couldn't believe it.

I told Cynthia that I had the feeling that somehow this reference to my grandma and Molly Brown would end up in my book, but I wondered how many people would even know about the musical from the 1960s. Cynthia not only was aware of it but also had sung one of the songs in her high school talent show for homecoming queen, and decades later, she included the event in her book, as experienced by her character Rose. I was awed by Mama's magical way to present a multifaceted message, which was later highlighted and heightened by Cynthia.

Well, I was mistaken to even consider that this chapter would end here, as the synchronicities continued to make their presence known. After tak-ing a nap on one very transformative day, I woke with Seal's song in my head again. It stayed with me for quite a while, even when I was trying to concentrate on other things.

That evening, I felt guided to watch a television documentary, *Da Vinci's Lost Code* (Discovery Times, March 17, 2007). My son had recorded it for me the week prior. It was about the source and meaning of a painting of two babies—either Jesus and John the Baptist or both the earthly and the Heavenly Jesus—meeting lips. The show questioned whether it had been painted by Leonardo da Vinci and, assuming it had been, explored its possible encoded message. The documentary also referred to Mary Magdalene.

It explored the theory that Leonardo da Vinci was portraying the ideas of the Cathars in his paintings. I hadn't heard of the Cathars until recent months. This prompted my discussions with others, and I further learned they were peaceful people, regarded as Gnostics, who believed that God was found in the heart and not in a building. I also discovered that the Cathars were thought to be guardians of the Holy Grail but were eventu-ally massacred for their beliefs.

At one point, when the narrator of the documentary said, "But the Cathars weren't alone in believing in the significance of a sacred kiss," there was a shot of yellow and red roses—another kiss and rose connection. The signs are mirroring what my intuition keeps telling me, that the kiss from a rose is indeed a sacred one—it appears to metaphorically represent being kissed by the Divine. When it was time to go to bed at the end of this very intense and magical day, I saw visions of roses in my third eye, the gateway to clairvoyance.

I kept hearing Seal's song on the radio. Such as, when my daughter suddenly asked to switch the dial to her new favorite radio station, none other than "Kiss from a Rose" was playing. And just prior to arriving home with her to find that my cross had gloriously reappeared after its mysterious disappearance, minutes before I would witness the miracle with my own eyes (as told in the chapter "Expect the Unexpected"), the song came on the car radio as well.

Weeks after the initial Molly Brown synchronicity, I did volunteer work at our school's fund-raiser, which included a silent auction. At one point during the evening, I perused the different items up for bidding. Suddenly I heard a woman across from me tell her friend that she had "to check out the Molly Brown House Museum." I interrupted, "Do you mean The *Unsinkable* Molly Brown?" She pointed to the auction bid for tickets to the Molly Brown House Museum in Denver and said, "Yes, The Unsinkable Molly Brown." I had never heard of the museum before, and I had forgotten that she had lived in Denver.

Other than seeing the character of Molly Brown portrayed in the movie Titanic *ten years ago, I cannot recall hearing or reading anything about her, the movie or the person, in more than thirty years—that is, until these recent weeks—and suddenly Molly was everywhere.*

The signs resurfaced yet again when my ex-husband took my kids to the library. While looking at the video selections, Jack pointed out only one movie to my daughter, saying she would like it. Yes, it was *The Unsinkable Molly Brown*. He had no clue about all my recent synchronicities surrounding it. I didn't even know that Jack had seen the movie before.

My kids and I eventually rented the movie. At one point, the top Denver socialite has her annual celebration when her "roses are in bloom." Oh, how that one line gave me goose pimples. I couldn't help but make the connection of Seal's song to a line in a movie made more than forty years ago—and, of course, I have been seeking any connections between this song and this musical since my grandmother's message.

To further overwhelm us with Titanic phenomena during this time, my kids and I also watched the 1997 version of *Titanic*. Although I had seen the movie a decade ago, I had forgotten the name of the female lead character who survives the sinking of the ship: *Rose*.

Soon thereafter, on an "uneventful" day comprised of another dental visit and a trip to the grocery store, I was driving from Boulder on my way home and was suddenly overcome with a strong knowingness. Something very synchronistic was about to occur, and I was being urged to be aware. Sure enough, the fun began when I saw the license plate on the car directly ahead of me. It read "TITANC." Of course, this made me think of that unsinkable Molly. I was surprised that there was a personalized license plate referring to the Titanic and that I "happened" to see it. But that was only the beginning.

Just as I noticed that the car ahead of it had a license plate with the numbers 444, the song "Hero" by Enrique Iglesias came on with the words "I can be your hero, baby." Again, there's that reference to being saved, as in the Molly Brown synchronicities.

The words that stood out in my mind in the very next song that played, "Cool Change," by Little River Band, were "When you're out on the sea alone." Well, Molly was out on the sea too. The song is, basically, about the need for change.

As I write this, Tracy Chapman's song "New Beginning" begins to play on my iTunes. She sings about the world being beyond fixing and how we should just start over. My ears wake up with the words "Create a new world."

Immediately following the song about change was a radio advertisement for the movie *Evening*. In the background was Dido's song "White Flag," which includes the surprising lyric "I will go down with this ship" as the person claims she will not surrender. Although this represents not being saved, I think the message is that we must surrender in order to be saved. All these songs and license plates, which came into my awareness in rapid succession, were about being saved, the power of God's love, heroism, surrender, and change.

Suddenly, I was getting a whole new interpretation of all the Molly Brown synchronicities. Just like the 9/11 synchronicities, I was at least somewhat regarding it on a personal level. However, these synchronicities seem to be reflecting global change. They are asking me to communicate in my own way that, although there is so much fear about the future of our earth, we will be saved and we must surrender to a Higher Power.

My mind then recalled the first extraordinary Chihuahua synchronicity, as described in the chapter "The Chihuahua Presence." Could it be that it was reflecting the very same message? I ran out of gas and somehow found safety following intense prayer right at The Big I, or perhaps The Big "Eye," symbolizing the Eye of God. I had no choice but to fully surrender to God's help. In that moment of being saved, I saw a truck with a huge picture of Christ on the cross. To further emphasize the message, I saved that little dog. All this happened after purchasing a book called *The Saving Graces* that very morning. What is all of this saying to me? Is it communicating that we're on that track toward being saved on earth, but we need to come together and allow for change by surrendering to God's grace?

A few weeks after spotting that Titanic license plate, my kids and I spontaneously (but I'm convinced my angels were urging me to) set out for the Denver Museum of Nature and Science. We wanted to attend none other than "Titanic: The Artifact Exhibition," a traveling exhibit at the museum, along with the IMAX movie *Ghosts of the Abyss*, also about the Titanic. How timely this was, considering my recent thread of synchronicities.

The song randomly playing on my iTunes as I write this is "Falling Slowly," by Glen Hansard and Marketa Irglova. I've listened to it forty times (as iTunes displays the number of times each song has been played), but not until this moment did I notice the words "Take this sinking boat and point it home"— an extremely relevant sign! To me, "home" refers to Heaven. Because Heaven will be what saves us.

We arrived at the museum in time to first see the exhibition and then go right to the last movie showing of the day. As we approached the exhibit, a volunteer handed each of us a card that replicated a Titanic boarding pass. On the back of each was a description of an actual passenger of the doomed ship. It gave the person's name, age, birthplace, class, starting point and destination, the reason for travel, and other passenger facts. We would find out, at the end of the tour, whether our person survived.

After we checked out each other's passes, I asked the volunteer if she had one that was Molly Brown's, as it would be very meaningful for me to have it. She told me she had never seen a Molly Brown pass before, probably because Molly was already so famous and the exhibitors wanted people to learn about the other passengers.

So off we went. When another attendant double-checked our tickets, I again felt compelled to ask her if she had seen any Molly Brown passes. I was feeling strangely assertive on this day. She gave me the same answer as the other woman. So I let the idea go, and off we went to the exhibit. As interested as I was in everything, I was feeling very spacey. I had to read every exhibit description about three times before I could comprehend it.

I had an awakening as I toured the exhibit. Years before I had these Molly Brown synchronicities, I had the awareness that, in a past life, I was on the Titanic. Although I had lifetimes where I was poor and starving, or where I had taken the vows of poverty, I also had lifetimes where I was very rich. Many of us have probably experienced both extremes. I married into wealth in this lifetime, and I did survive the Titanic, as did most women in first class on the ship. We have all had so many lifetimes, and perhaps because of the extreme trauma associated with this particular one, I forced the awareness of it away from me as quickly as it had come. However, it suddenly came rushing back from my subconscious into conscious awareness on this day.

When I stood by a picture and description of Molly Brown and read that her maiden name was "Margaret Tobin" and that she was the wife of James Joseph (J. J.) Brown, I asked Scott for his boarding pass. It was Molly's! Scott had received Molly Brown's boarding pass (see photo), and two employees didn't even think it existed. We were so surprised that Scott had hers all along!

I couldn't believe that I hadn't recognized the pass as hers, but I saw "Margaret Tobin" and didn't make the connection. I'd noticed that the passenger was from Denver and—well, frankly, I really can't explain my thinking. I'd been spaced-out ever since our arrival to the exhibit.

Interestingly, my daughter's passenger ticket also had the last name "Brown," but this woman was from South Africa. Considering that less than one-third of the passengers survived the disaster, we were surprised that all three of our passengers had survived. This mirrored the constant theme of being saved. As I've explained in previous chapters, our subconscious will bring up, with the help of synchronicity, what we need to heal, including past lives. I believe this is one of the many reasons for the Molly Brown synchronicities, but, as I've said, things can happen for even a million reasons.

When I was a little girl and my grandma took me to see the musical *The Unsinkable Molly Brown*, that was just the beginning of the unfolding in this lifetime. I do believe my spirit existed in someone on that ship and did survive, although it was not Molly. But that has such small significance to the monumental meaning behind the Molly Brown synchronicities.

I now see that we, the billions of us on the planet, have metaphorically been passengers on the Titanic. We have indeed been sinking; but we will be saved. We must surrender to a Higher Power. We must trust that we will indeed have peace on earth as well as a healed earth. We must believe that this will occur no matter *what* is going on, *even if things keep getting worse before they change.*

This is all coming together, as I write these words. However, I don't feel that I am the only one writing this. I am now convinced of the significance of Molly and the rose! The Molly Brown and Titanic synchronicities are truly about our salvation, as the whole world *is* being saved from the disaster we have collectively created—the wars, the hatred, the famine, the exploitation of and irreverence toward the environment and people—all of it. We *are* unsinkable. We *are* being saved by surrendering to God. We do this by moving toward greater spiritual connection as we recognize God's awesome grace. Ultimately, we surrender to love.

The rose synchronicities are about the Divine feminine energy, the energy represented by Mary Magdalene, which is pervading our consciousness, as per our collective intentions, to dissolve the greed, corruption, war, and destruction that free will created but that can no longer resonate energetically on our evolving planet. The rose *is* in bloom. We *are* being kissed by the Divine.

No wonder my grandmother was showing me the connection between Molly and the rose. They are together, metaphorically, the window to our new and chosen destiny.

Months after I completed this chapter, I learned about the ship that struck ice off Antarctica and began to sink, but passengers took to lifeboats and were amazingly rescued by a passing cruise ship ("Cruise ship sinks off Antarctica; all OK" USA Today, *November 23, 2007). All were saved from the sinking ship! Just like the Titanic, this ship hit ice. I consider this to be an astounding metaphor. Here is yet another synchronistic connection that supports this monumental message I keep receiving in many ways—except this is with real people being saved from a real sinking ship!*

Days after reading this news report, I was guided to go online to check my local news. I saw the headline, "Denver woman among survivors of Antarctica disaster." I thought of former Denver resident Molly Brown and pondered the synchronistic connection. I then opened up the article and in the very first sentence a connection was made between Molly Brown and this woman who was saved, expressing that she, too, "is definitely unsinkable" (www.dailycamera.com, November 28, 2007).

After reading the article, I shared this news with my daughter. Karen told me that her teacher talked about the sinking ship during class today. She went on to explain, "He said it's like the second Titanic except that everyone was saved." Yes, and so shall we all be saved.

CHAPTER 19

A NEW WAY OF LIVING

You must be the change you wish to see in the world.
—Mahatma Gandhi

*W*e are being driven to change our world, beginning with each of us on an individual level. This requires a personal, intentional shift in our own paradigm, one that causes us to look first to ourselves for positive change. We reconnect with our authentic selves, as spiritual beings, living from the inside out, rather than from the outside in. When we intend to act in this manner, we find that synchronicities support us by illuminating our lives so that we find a new way of living that is conducive to providing this shift: helping us to release what no longer serves us, moving us toward healing, providing new opportunities, and constantly blessing us with guidance and grace.

Taking Responsibility for Our Lives and Creating Anew

An evolution in the way we view and experience life begins with our awareness that we truly do create our lives. We fully attract our life experience through our thoughts, feelings, words, and actions (as well as spiritual tests, challenges that we choose in inter-life, and those experiences accrued by way of karmic retribution). This is what we are being asked to acknowledge. The popularity of the movie *The Secret* shows that many are indeed awakening to the concept of conscious creation.

Those who do accept this concept as their truth need to release any attachments to victimhood, guilt, and self-blame. We must realize that the subconscious mind holds all memories, 24/7, of everything that has ever happened to each of us in this life and in our past lives, which can create our deep-seated beliefs. These beliefs, both positive and negative, control us like computer software. Many of these beliefs are formed in childhood.

For instance, if a young girl is told by her teacher that her schoolwork is not good enough, this one harmful statement can create a belief about her young self, and she could live as "not good enough" for the rest of her life. The young mind hasn't yet developed the ability to reason and defend itself, and thus those words go right to her subconscious mind and are regarded as truth. This misbelief can unknowingly pervade all areas of her future life, causing her to be "not good enough" in her relationships, her work, her connection to God—everything. Conversely, positive words spoken to her as a child would drop into her subconscious, as well, which become positive beliefs that would positively affect her future as a woman.

If a father is in a bad mood and takes it out on his little boy by saying, "You'll never amount to anything," the child may end up leading an unsuccessful life. He could be a genius, gifted with an array of talents and abilities; however, as an adult, his career may not ever get off the ground, and he may never live up to his potential, because of the belief system that is running him. Misbeliefs are controlling and will attract people, situations, and things that support the negative self-thoughts one forms at a tender age. This boy's young mind can't comprehend that his father's comment had nothing to do with the truth, that the man merely took his frustrations and own insecurities out on his son. Coming from an authority figure and role model, the father's words actually become the child's truth. Our words are extremely powerful.

When studying hypnotherapy, I learned about the workings of the subconscious mind and realized to my surprise just how powerful all words are—and not just in the mind of the child. I learned that words spoken during surgery or in emergency situations, even when the person is unconscious, are fully heard and recorded by the patient's subconscious mind. This is why it is so important that emergency technicians, doctors, surgeons, and all support staff watch their words and thoughts during these situations.

If a patient's subconscious hears how bad or hopeless the prognosis is during surgery, it can potentially have a negative effect on the outcome. Listening to music that is comforting and exudes positive energy while in surgery, if allowed, is advantageous even though the patient isn't consciously aware of the sounds. When one is in an emergency state or in a coma, speaking positive, encouraging, and loving words to the patient is extremely beneficial.

Our subconscious minds are recording everything, even prior to incarnation and during the birth process. The birth experience itself can dictate belief systems the person will carry as he or she matures. For instance, babies born by cesarean section can live, even throughout adulthood, with the belief that life is too easy, which could unknowingly create the opposite—a more difficult life. After all, they didn't have to go through the hard work of traveling through the birth canal, and they may hold that belief system until it is released through the subconscious mind.

Babies born normally may hold beliefs such as "I'm nothing special" or "My life is just routine." Babies born late may retain subconscious scripts such as "I'm a late bloomer" or "Everything is so long and hard for me." They may often be late to parties, meetings, or gatherings. Conversely, a premature delivery can create misbeliefs including "I'm not enough" or "There's not enough time for me." They may arrive to events early.

Indeed, the subconscious mind sets up our life challenges even as we are beginning our lives. Because this part of us creates easily and unknowingly in so many ways such as those described above, the results are often less than desirable. However, there is another side to this coin. The good news is that we can heal and release the negative self-thoughts we acquired in our youth, in addition to our birth scripts; one technique is described later in this chapter. We can then intend new, supporting, and positive beliefs that replace the misbeliefs, as defined in the next chapter "Choose Again." With courage and wisdom, we take responsibility for the fact that we create our own lives and then we can learn to become our own healers, as well as conscious creators.

Only in recent years have I begun to understand on a deep level, through hypnotherapy, why I wasn't attracting money despite my conscious desires. Achieving financial wealth simply did not mesh with my beliefs on a subconscious level—those false, deep-seated thoughts that were controlling me, such as "Money and God don't mix" or "Money is the root of all evil." I couldn't acquire something I unknowingly despised; my subconscious mind would not allow it.

I recalled my past lifetimes as a nun and a monk, those times when I took the vows of poverty (and chastity, too). These vows were stamped onto my way of being throughout many incarnations. Some of my hypnotherapy clients found similar kinds of connections with regard to beliefs about money, as well as sex. They too were connected to vows they'd made in previous lifetimes.

When the miracle of awareness is ready to present itself, we learn to release and heal negative memories and beliefs and shift toward consciously creating anew. As our awareness reveals that the power of our thoughts, feelings, words, and actions are either bringing us closer to or taking us further from our deepest longings, new choices are made.

As Gandhi said, "Always aim at complete harmony of thought and word and deed. Always aim at purifying your thoughts and everything will be well." When you get your feelings behind everything, you naturally create the harmony with what you think, say, and do. Get your feelings fully behind your longings.

For example, if you desire to find a mate, imagine those feelings of being in love—having someone to share life with, to grow with, to touch and be touched by, to kiss and be kissed by—and just fully feel as if you are in love. When you watch a great love story on film, imagine yourself in your own story about a great love. When you see a happy couple walking hand in hand, imagine yourself as having that in your life, having the gift of giving and receiving love, and explore what that feels like. If this practice causes discomfort or negative thoughts to arise, these feelings and thoughts need to be addressed.

We can choose to think, feel, say, and do things in new and supportive ways, form more positive beliefs, and create consciously. We breathe gratitude into every aspect of this creative process. The Universe then steps in to fulfill our requests through the power of synchronicity, which weaves through all aspects of our lives to provide the opportunities, guidance, and validation we require to create. This is co-creation. We work in tandem with God for ultimate conscious creation.

Marching to Your Own Drummer

I could write a whole book about all the things I've done to please others and society. The pressure I felt to mirror everyone else's opinions and actions was too powerful. It took me years to wake up and just be who I am; to not care so much about what others think of me, and to be careful of what I feed my mind by considering what I read, what I do, what I allow myself to be exposed to, and with whom I spend my time. I eventually learned to be a more educated consumer and not blindly buy unhealthy and dangerous foods, just because we're bombarded with unsafe choices. I learned to look beyond mainstream medicine for vital, preventative health information, and gain awareness of the consequences of unhealthy and dangerous product use. Since my spiritual awakening, I've increasingly recognized the need to make new choices.

As we march to our own drummer, we wake from the slumber of mechanically following others and become more mindful, educated, and aware. In order to do this, we find the courage and creativity to make new choices and consider new ways of being.

For instance, do we really want to be accessible to the world 24/7 via our cell phones, which interrupt our meals, our conversations with our spouses and children, and our much-needed down time? Or is it that society expects us to be available at all times of the day no matter what the unseen costs? Many of us jump on the "I'm here for you at all times" bandwagon, a habit that is difficult to break for social and professional reasons.

On top of that, and much more importantly, the billions of EMF (electromagnetic fields)-radiating cell phones in use on this planet, as well as cordless phones, are considered by a growing number of people to be very dangerous. Some are also concerned about the usage of microwave ovens, which are known to alter the chemical structure of our food. However, the potential dangers posed by these products are suppressed. The truths are coming out, slowly but surely. We now have protection for my family's cell phones so we can still benefit from the convenience and access for family communication (for information, go to www.marysoliel.com). We lived with a regular oven and corded phones before, and we are living with them again.

We can also learn to live with natural sweeteners such as stevia. Many of us regularly ingest artificial sweeteners with misleading, safe-sounding names, because they are found in such a wide variety of products and so many in our society consume them. Even though we hear about their potentially serious health risks, it's hard for us to wake up to the deception, because millions of us are hooked on them.

Because we are constantly seduced by many large corporations' sugar-laden beverages, fast-food restaurants, and an endless number of overprocessed food products with high-fat and high-sugar contents, we are often unaware of, or at least numb to, their true hazards. Is the overriding belief that because everyone is consuming them, they must be okay for us? We lead such busy lives, and these products solve our problems of time constraints with meal preparation.

We often follow the norm not only with what we purchase, consume, and use in our daily existence but also with what we do. Is it in our elementary school-age children's best interest to sign them up for so many after-school activities, classes, and sports that they become busier than we adults are, because that's what all the other parents are doing? Isn't this causing our children to become overstressed and exhausted? Aren't our children growing up too fast? Don't they need more down time?

The emphasis placed on our middle and high schoolers' clothes, body types, and looks seems to far exceed the importance placed on their character, goodness, and integrity. Peer pressure is a more powerful force than ever, and children who don't look or act "right" according to teenage society standards are suffering ridicule and abhorrent attacks on their potentially fragile self-esteems.

Adults, too, feel pressure to look right. They also want to fit in, just as kids do. Why isn't there more emphasis on the beauty of who we all really are and what we contribute to the world? For those of us who don't measure up and think we fall short of society's expectations, how much mental energy is wasted on worrying about what others think? As an overweight woman, I can strongly attest to this wasteful practice.

Synchronicity has illuminated this new way of seeing things. I realized we all have the choice to navigate through life by listening to either Divine guidance or society. Because I chose the former, at least most of the time, I have a knowingness of how to best spend my time. I attract those things that resonate with my higher choices and preferences. When I veer off the road, which inevitably occurs, I proactively choose again. When I follow my guidance, I feel happier, healthier, and confident.

The right information falls into my lap, just at the right time, helping me to be a more educated consumer. I am often drawn to just the right wellness professionals, who enlighten me with their expertise. Products that fight the toxins we are all exposed to from our air, water, and food, as well as the electromagnetic pollution affecting the body's energy field, come into my awareness.

I have barely skimmed the surface of what I need to know about achieving ultimate health and learning about safe and unsafe product choices, but I'm moving in the right direction. If my food choices aren't beneficial, I know I can count on signs to reveal them and cause me to make better choices. For example, if I ordered a diet cola and the waiter told me that they "just ran out," I would not deem that a coincidence. I would want to understand the synchronistic message. The fact is, artificial sweeteners don't agree with me, and I finally, after many years, recognized and accepted the conclusions coming from various studies that they are dangerous, so I no longer consume them.

Buffering Our Reactions

Our reactions to life's challenges become slower, wiser, more contemplative, and hold much less tension as we adopt a more spiritual way of being. We see things from a higher perspective and don't get as easily upset. This single practice prevents further undesirable creations. Even if someone yells at us, instead of yelling right back, we look at what is behind the anger. We choose to be more even-keeled and laid back and to live more peacefully.

This doesn't usually happen overnight. It takes practice, and as we become more in line with our highest interests, we gain more wisdom, and it becomes easier and actually empowering to buffer our reactions. However, anger can be healthy and necessary. We cannot allow anyone to walk all over us. Sometimes we need to get upset first so that we can let go of our anger. And oftentimes we need to tell the people who hurt us about our pain so that they understand our feelings.

Holding on to the emotional pain can translate into real physical pain and imbalances in the body, which can possibly, over time, create disease. This is one reason why emotions must not be ignored—ever. Also, if you always stifle your feelings and anger toward others, you're basically telling the Universe that you're okay with receiving poor treatment and being a punching bag. When you communicate with the people who have hurt you, they may or may not own up and take responsibility, and sometimes you need to communicate spirit to spirit.

Regardless, the next vital step is allowing yourself to release the negativity, because otherwise it hurts only you. Then you can have true freedom: forgiveness. It becomes a relief on all levels to release the charge. In the heat of the battle, the struggle never feels good, no matter who is right or wrong.

Synchronicity will always reveal to you what and with whom you need to release. Often, the Universe will bring the two of you together, perhaps through an unexpected meeting, or you will receive the message through a dream or a series of signs. By heeding these messages, you can move forward in your life and release the heavy baggage that may weigh you down.

To prevent future baggage or negative effects from being created and accumulating in your life, there is a simple practice that can alter the outcome, regarding our negative words and thoughts. Any time we speak or think things we wish we hadn't, we can negate them by saying or thinking, "cancel, cancel" or whatever words work best for you. With your feelings behind the words, you will transmute the negative energy.

For instance, if a woman in her forties starts noticing changes in her body and acknowledges them by saying, "Oh, I'm getting old," she's putting that belief out there. She's telling her cells that she is indeed aging and is focusing on signs of aging. What you think, you become.

She can talk to her cells and slow the aging process with a new attitude and way of being. She can reverse this at any time by merely canceling out the negative thoughts about aging, accepting the natural and positive aspects of it, and choosing again. There are people in their eighties that act and feel younger than others in their forties—it's all about choice, attitude, and perspective.

By the way, it is said that our physical bodies are capable of living much longer than they do, but our collective beliefs regarding the human life span prevent us from living beyond a certain age, typically in the nineties and early hundreds. I know of a doctor who, when asked how old he is, says he is "ageless," as he chooses not to make the connection.

If a teenager begins every day with thoughts of hating school, he will, through the Law of Attraction, create negative circumstances that will match his beliefs and reinforce the idea that school is indeed something to be despised. However, if he cancels out these thoughts as they occur, and proactively thinks positively about his school life, he may then attract great friends, a new club to join that excites him, and good, fair teachers, for example. When he regresses to old ways of thinking when he inevitably has a bad day, he can immediately take notice and cancel them out. Soon, the positive thoughts become more commonplace.

The same goes for those times when one is in the midst of complaining. Once that person realizes that her focus on her frustrations will only perpetuate the annoyances, with new faces and events, she learns to stop the negative talk and "cancel, cancel" it out.

Let's examine the common frustration many of us share from time to time: the reckless, thoughtless, and incompetent drivers on the road. We can choose to see and react to these experiences in a new way. If we are really honest with ourselves, we will admit that we may have driven just as poorly as these fellow beings at least at some times in our lives.

I realize that I'm guilty of many of the acts for which I've gotten upset at other drivers: I've followed a car too close, failed to let someone in when I should have, and cut someone off. Even if these acts were unintentional, I still did these things, and I can't just assume that someone else is intentionally driving too close, for example. I've learned to just get off the road or move to the next lane if I'm not comfortable with the driver behind me. Sure, I get upset at times, especially if the car behind me is dangerously and recklessly close, but my reactions are healthier overall.

This point was mirrored to me recently when a lady dangerously merged in front of me, just missing my car, and then, about three blocks down the road, got all upset with her arms flailing around when another driver did the same to her.

This example can be applied to all aspects of our lives. We all experience frustration and anger when things go wrong. The way we handle these feelings is what directs the quality of our lives. Synchronicity always steps in to show us the way.

Stepping into Our Magnificence

Our deepest fear is not that we are inadequate. Our deepest fear is that we are powerful beyond measure. It is our light, not our darkness, that frightens us most.
—Marianne Williamson, from *A Return to Love*

Do we dare allow ourselves to realize that we are so grand? As we increasingly connect to who we really are, spiritual beings, this realization causes us to recognize that we truly are powerful beyond belief. That can be quite scary.

When you come to recognize and then tap into your endless potential, the Universe steps in to illuminate the possibilities and support you every step of the way. As that happens, fears no longer paralyze you, because you realize that you are not alone and that you have this invaluable support and guidance. You take the necessary actions to achieve your new goals. As more and more people step into their magnificence, particularly with positions that positively serve others, global transformation occurs.

In order to create Heaven on earth, we are becoming more spiritually aligned as a whole. As more and more of us recognize our magnificence, we work in tandem with the Universe. This becomes a catalyst for others. It is believed that the shift into a Heavenly earth doesn't require the participation of the majority of people. This shift starts with a very small percentage of people, a critical mass, which then causes more to awaken to a new way of living and being.

Embracing Change

We learn to accept that which commonly gives most of us discomfort—change. Change is constant, and we are learning to embrace it rather than fear it. In order to embrace change, we must release the need for attachment. The less we are attached to various things in our lives, the more easily we can adapt to the new. As you consciously pursue the spiritual path, watch for synchronicity to illuminate this necessary step.

As we experience change with less resistance, we recognize that our many attachments were a heavy weight to bear. Releasing this weight as much as possible from all levels of your being will make you feel lighter. You will live from a higher state of thinking and being. This will unlock the door to exciting new possibilities and opportunities that are in line with your highest interests.

In order to raise our vibrations, we need to let go of parts of ourselves that no longer serve us. If one realizes she must let go of her need to create constant drama in her life, for example, even though this will greatly benefit her future life, this is still a part of her, and when she lets it go she may grieve on some level. Letting go of parts of ourselves can be the most challenging changes we make. The process may create temporary sadness, but this type of change is necessary and will improve our lives in ways we cannot imagine.

New Choices That Reflect Who We Are

As we seek more authenticity in our lives, we are drawn to those we best resonate with, on a deeper level. It gets increasingly difficult to have idle chitchat when our souls are asking for deeper connections. As we attract more important soul relationships, superficial friendships or associations between people on different levels pale in comparison, and we feel restless and frustrated with them. Once this is recognized and accepted, things naturally readjust as you attract new connections. These connections will be with people who support your passion, who aren't in competition with you, and who are in line with who you are.

So, if you consistently have difficulty meeting up with a friend or an acquaintance—whether someone keeps canceling, the weather won't cooperate, or one of you forgets—the Universe could be mirroring something to you. Maybe the time just isn't right, but the message should be honored with no fault attributed to either party; the expenditure of time and energy isn't in your highest interest, perhaps for just a particular length of time.

The same thing goes for the activities we choose. We are seeking activities that fulfill us on a deeper level. We attract those things into our lives that nourish our souls and that we are passionate about, whether these things include art, music, mountain climbing, or scuba diving—whatever expressions that connect us to who we really are.

As we connect more to our authentic selves, many of us are finding a new balance in everything. We are taking breaks from the complexities of our advancing, technologically based society in order to find joy in the simpler things and feel more, to be in conscious touch with our feelings.

We may be pulled toward a greater appreciation of nature, as our connection to the earth expands. We seek out beauty in the real and natural; although beauty can also be found in the artificial and synthetic, especially through signs. We call forth more synchronicities, and, because we are more attuned to the earth, we can better recognize and honor them.

Recognizing "Enough-ness"

Even though "enough-ness" is not a word, please allow me to use it to demonstrate the benefits of living from a perceptual state of having enough rather than one of need or lack. When we focus on "not-enough-ness," that is just what we attract: not enough of what we desire. Rather, we can choose to maintain the mind-set that we have more than enough and see the Universe as abundant and always serving us.

When you refuse to see a lack of love, joy, success, or finances but rather concentrate on gratitude for what you do have in these areas, the Universe responds by providing more of that which you appreciate in your life, as you visualize, think, and feel your way into manifestation.

For example, let's look at this on a very simple level. If your vase holds one rose, treasuring that rose and emphasizing joy and gratitude for the beautiful flower will only attract more of the same. However, if you think, "It's *only* one rose," your focus is on not having enough. Because what you focus on expands, you will keep receiving that which you deem is not enough.

As you recognize synchronicity in your life and get excited about and grateful for it, you will be graced with even more. This will translate into creating the life you desire, a life with enough-ness. This infinite source of blessings will shower you with the spiritual gift of positive illumination when you choose to live as an abundant being who does not think in terms of lack.

Feeding the Body, Mind, and Soul

In the United States, which is an overfed yet undernourished country, we are in need of finding proper ways of nourishing our bodies. We are constantly overwhelmed by an endless array of unhealthy choices. Of course, the big money of corporations gets in the way, and we often hear conflicting reports on what is good or bad for us. And it sometimes seems as if things have to get really bad before they can swing to the other side.

For instance, over the years, soda and junk food machines have been placed in several schools across the nation. How could this constant and easy access not cause some of our kids to become even more addicted to sugar and junk food? Only when we finally recognized the serious obesity epidemic among our kids (sugar and junk food consumption being among the main culprits), have we been forced to recognize the need to ban these unhealthy products in schools altogether.

We now have a national trend that forbids foods that don't meet certain nutritional criteria. However, we still have kids who are used to consuming high amounts of sugar and junk food on a daily basis. The title of an article in my local paper is very telling: "Sugar High: Boulder's new school nutrition rules turn junk food into black-market booty" (Boulder Weekly, November 8-14, 2007). These kids who are used to consuming these products now have the task of relearning how to eat properly.

For all of us, the bottom line is, we each know intuitively what is good for our bodies—for every part of us, for that matter. We just have to get quiet enough and tune in. As we become increasingly turned off by over-processed and sugar-laden foods and drawn to more whole foods that nature provides, we begin to understand that our physical bodies indeed are what we eat. We can also attract, through synchronicity, proper and truthful information and become educated, as well as intuitive, consumers.

Nature also provides what we need to supplement ourselves to heal as well as to maintain good health. As reflected in the following portrayal, some may agree that we have come full circle in our ways of healing:

The History of Medicine:

2000 BC   "Here, eat this root."

AD 1000   "That root is heathen. Here, say this prayer."

AD 1850   "That prayer is superstition. Here, drink this potion."

AD 1940   "That potion is snake oil. Here, swallow this pill."

AD 1985   "That pill is ineffective. Here, take this antibiotic."

AD 2000   "That antibiotic is unhealthy. Here, eat this root."
            —Anonymous

Perhaps Thomas Edison's prediction, made decades ago, will come true: "The doctor of the future will give no medicine, but will interest his patients in the care of the human frame, in diet, and in the cause and prevention of disease." More wisdom came from Florence Nightingale, the founder of modern nursing, who said, "Nature alone cures ... and what nursing has to do is put the patient in the best condition for nature to act upon them."

Our bodies are begging us to take a proactive stance, to become more preventative with our health, instead of just reactive. More of us are moving toward taking control of our own health and away from putting Band-Aids on our symptoms, while still utilizing and blessing mainstream medicine when necessary and in conjunction with natural and alternative ways of healing and maintaining our health. We truly are in the driver's seat of our own destiny; we are not victims to it.

For the health of our minds, we spend more time with things that uplift us rather than deplete us. It's a relief to maintain optimism rather than dwelling on what's wrong with the world, a very difficult and challenging task these days. I am curious to see how news reporting evolves as we evolve. Will the networks report in a responsible manner and include more news about what's right with the world instead of perpetuating the negative and building intense fears about our present and future?

I cannot imagine that the 24/7 reporting of primarily negative news, which results in the building of fear within the masses, will continue as we move toward a universal understanding of how we create our reality. Will we continue to be teased and provoked into staying up for the ten o'clock news to find out about what new dangers are lurking inside and just outside our homes, building up our daily stress levels, or will we be informed in a balanced, truthful, and inspiring way?

When there is a natural or man-made disaster, will the reporting of it be communicated and sensationalized with the use of dramatic music and immediately created, impressive graphics, or will the story be reported responsibly and with the utmost respect toward those affected? Will we care as much about the headline story about the latest celebrity breakup? Or will we concentrate on what's happening in our own lives?

For our spiritual health, we move toward anything that lifts our spirits, whether that be engaging in positive discussions, listening to music, talking to our angels, meditating, reading uplifting material, attending a workshop, or any of the endless possibilities. When we find ourselves weary or challenged from the stressors of life, we counter these difficulties with actions that realign us spiritually.

The health of our bodies, minds, and souls must together be addressed, because they are deeply connected. If one's mind holds constant negative thoughts, for example, the energy of those thoughts may eventually create disease or "dis-ease" of the physical body. In addition, if one is spiritually depleted, the body and mind can be drained as well. By striving toward balance, with awareness of disruption in any of our systems, we achieve ultimate and all-around health. We adopt a more natural way of health maintenance and prevention that addresses all levels of our being in a balanced manner.

Being Proactive in Transmuting Energy

As we grow our realization that everything has energy, we develop the awareness of those energies that aren't conducive to our own and then clear them. We become proactive. For instance, if a chicken was raised in poor conditions, it becomes food that carries the negative energy of what the chicken endured. Or if the chef at a restaurant is in an angry place while preparing a meal, that food takes on his energy as well. However, we can change the nature of this energy, as it can be transmuted with our mere intention. We can remind ourselves of Emoto's *Messages From Water* for a dose of confidence in the power of our words and thoughts. We can also count on synchronicity and intuition to make us aware of those things that need to be cleared.

Of course, the same goes for our own emotional state when we're around food. If we get angry with our mate at the dinner table or shame a child into eating a certain way, the food takes on those energies. Additionally, the negative emotion can be connected to an actual food, and that child or adult may develop an allergy to it. My healer, Dr. Sie, initially taught my children and me to always maintain happy and positive conversations at the dinner table, and this comes quite easily for us. But if something suddenly occurs, such as upsetting news or a distressing phone call, dinner will be delayed.

I recall standing in a line in a deli where you custom order a sandwich. The young man preparing my meal appeared to be new to his job and had a hard time putting my sandwich together but I was very patient with him. His manager interrupted and in an angry manner demonstrated the correct procedure, strongly chiding and belittling his employee for his performance while slapping slices of meat together onto the bread. Because I didn't want to make the situation worse for the employee, I ate that sandwich (after clearing the negative energy) even though I lost my appetite. In hindsight, I wished I had just walked out.

Subconsciously, we can make positive and negative associations between various things. If we are eating popcorn while watching a violent movie, it is possible to become allergic to corn. If a well-meaning mother pops a sucker into the mouth of her screaming child after a vaccination, that child can, at least subconsciously, make the connection between the "sweet" and the "pain," and, here too, an allergy can possibly develop.

Before drinking or eating, we can send positive thoughts to our food and water, something like, "Thank you for this healthful food and water" or "I am grateful that this healthfully meets my physical needs." This not only will help on an energetic level but also is a beautiful way to show gratitude for our nourishment—a prayer of thanks combined with an energetic infusion of positive thoughts.

Sometimes we are energetically affected by things that have nothing to do with choice or action. As strange as this may sound, people can attach to us energetically and drain us. If you feel tired and drained and have no reason to feel this way, it could be because someone has unconsciously attached an energetic cord (or cords) to you.

Having energetic cords attached to you is like having weeds in your garden. You don't want them around and should remove them. They can be from your husband, ex-wife, friend, or co-worker—any of your present relationships—or even from past relationships or those who have passed on. These cords can be "cut" with your intention either while you're fully aware or when you're deep in meditation or hypnosis. You can also ask your angels to handle this for you by asking them "to cut any cords attached to my body" or "to cut any cords I have attached to others." Cutting the cord(s) will remove only the unhealthy aspect of the relationship, as energy ceases to be drained from the individual. Then, imagine healing energy on those areas of the bodies where the cords were attached.

When I would lead a client or class in a meditation that would have them imagine themselves seated across from one who is attaching cords to them, or vice versa, many could tell you how many cords there were and where on the body they were attached. Without consciously knowing what was happening, those they were releasing cords from would feel the release in some way. On a couple of occasions, participants received a cell phone call from the other person immediately after the meditation.

I have since found that this process can be very simple and immediate. You can perform it while fully aware and in just a moment's time. If I intuit that there is a cord that needs to be removed, I muscle test to confirm. This is quick and easy way to verify their existence, but you can also tell by just noticing those times you feel drained and intuitively checking for attachments with others. I suggest googling *energetic cords* to find out more about this practice.

There are many wonderful healers who can help you cut energetic cords or release your misbeliefs and then strengthen you for new and supportive beliefs. We sometimes need others to help us with our struggles, blocks, and issues. I go to other healers from time to time, for help with working on myself when I get stuck. However, you can also empower yourself to become your own healer.

Becoming Your Own Healer

Ultimately, we heal ourselves, because we are absolutely capable of it in many ways. We heal through unconditional love and forgiveness, as discussed earlier. We also energetically release what no longer serves us. Just as the earth naturally does, often through weather activity, we need to keep clearing our own negative energy. On a personal level, we must clear out misbeliefs, pain, anger, and grudges, and then forgive and let go. Sometimes that includes relationships that no longer serve us. We continually clear out unhealthy mental chatter and negative self-thoughts. We also literally clear out things we don't need or use in our physical life, to unclutter our lives and make room for the new.

When there is something you know you need to clear out of your inner being, you can release it, again with your intention. Perhaps you are aware of a negative self-thought you hold or the negative effects of a past hurt. You can clear it by expressing the very powerful statement with absolute conviction:

"I release [state the misbelief or negative effects of an issue, event, or person] from every cell, from every muscle, tissue, and organ in my body, from every strand of DNA, from every fiber of my being. I fully release this now."

When I used to guide hypnotherapy clients through this kind of release while they were in trance, it seemed particularly effective, because the client would be in such a relaxed state that the subconscious could easily be redirected. Yet as we raise our vibrations and release what no longer serves us, healing is becoming easier at the conscious level. We can state our intentions for release of unwanted emotional energy, just as we can change the energy of our food and water. Try it for yourself, and you be the judge. Be aware of how you feel immediately following the release.

As I clear myself energetically, with my intention, I send the negative energy (imagine it) upward, because the earth has enough to deal with. The most beautiful part of releasing negative energy from ourselves is that the more we do this, the easier we can access our super-conscious minds, which is the ultimate goal.

There is an aspect of God in each of us, which resides in our super-conscious minds. This is the Divine part of us that knows unconditional love and forgiveness, as well as healing, grace, wisdom, infinite potential, and Universal intelligence. When each one of us taps into this place and lives more and more from this higher state of being, we raise our vibrations, and this positively affects the world as a whole.

Once the energetic clearing has taken place, you strengthen yourself by choosing the reverse of that negative thought. One way you can achieve this is through the creation of new beliefs through the power of affirmations, as revealed in the next chapter "Choose Again." Once you change the belief, you want to match it with what you think, feel, say, and do.

Embracing the Mysterious

Albert Einstein said, "The most beautiful experience we can have is the mysterious." I wholeheartedly agree. Every part of my being intends to be immersed in the mysteries and the magic; I want to know where I come from, my real home, while experiencing life on this planet. This is my great passion, to understand and experience the mysterious, the real truth. This is the food for my soul, and it lessens my deeper sadness, my homesickness for our true home. I may get only pockets of awareness, but I always desire more.

"We don't know a millionth of one percent about anything," said Thomas Edison. I feel this couldn't be truer than when we're seeking understanding of the unseen, what is going on behind the scenes of our own reality. We're never going to understand everything, as our human minds are incapable of it. Even when we reside in the Heavenly realms, I believe we are also on a journey to understanding and growth. Part of embracing the mysterious is surrendering to the process and not any kind of destination.

When we embrace the mysterious, we attract more of its presence. The more we attract, the more of Heaven we bring onto this earth and the higher our own vibrations become. As we reach to our angels and are willing to receive their gifts, the veil continues to thin, and our experiences and understandings become so much more profound. By embracing the mysterious, we more fully realize who we really are while still honoring and enjoying our humanness, a most desirable state of being.

The Choice Is Ours

Each of us can choose to empower ourselves and proactively create a new way of living. We can recognize and attract synchronicity, utilize our intuition, make new choices, embrace our ability to transmute energy in everything we encounter, and heal ourselves, all while continuing to embrace gratitude, unconditional love, and forgiveness. By practicing these things, we come to realize that we truly are powerful beyond belief.

CHAPTER 20

CHOOSE AGAIN

When your thoughts, feelings, words, and actions are creating undesirable results, you can choose again. First, misbeliefs and memories held on a subconscious level can be cleared and released with your intention, as discussed in the previous chapter. You can then re-create with new, supportive, and positive beliefs.

Listed on the following pages are examples of common unsupportive thought forms and negative belief patterns that can hold people back. Most of these originate from our past and others are newly acquired as adults. When you live and breathe a new, supporting belief, miracles begin to take place. These new statements can be spoken every day as affirmations, as many times a day as possible, and for as long as you feel the practice is necessary. Repetition is one way to reverse the undesirable negative self-thoughts held at the subconscious level.

Rewrite affirmations as you choose so they resonate best with you. Be sure to make your statements as brief as possible and with no negative words such as *never* or *not*. Instead of saying, "I am not going to be unhappy," for example, simple say, "I am happy." You also don't want the energy of the word/thought *unhappy* attached to you. Place written affirmations where you will always be reminded of them, such as on your bathroom mirror or nightstand, or on sticky notes placed all over your house.

Those moments before you fall asleep and before you fully wake up are particularly powerful times for you to speak these affirmations and redirect your subconscious mind. It is extremely important to feel self-love while speaking the new thoughts.

Once out of bed, stand before your reflection in the mirror and look directly into your own eyes as you speak the new beliefs with absolute conviction. Feel deeply what you speak, and breathe gratitude into your new creation. Then take the appropriate actions that support your healthy new thoughts and beliefs. If you slip up, be persistent and absolutely relentless about getting back on track.

Remember that even though you may not consciously hold these negative beliefs about yourself, you may on a subconscious level because of what occurred in your childhood or past lives. The first two misbeliefs mentioned are particularly common negative self-thoughts brought on during childhood. Allow your intuition to reveal anything that needs to be released, and then choose again. Synchronicity will reflect these new thoughts and direct positive change to take place.

Old: I am unlovable.
New: I am completely lovable.

Forgive yourself for anything you need to. Concentrate on all the things you love about yourself. When you love yourself completely, others will be attracted to you and reflect that love you already feel for yourself. Connect with God, and breathe in all the beauty that you are. The fact is, you are a child of God, and you are completely lovable.

Old: I am not good enough.
New: I am more than good enough.

There is no one in this world just like you. Realize that you have something special to offer that no one else can. Spend time doing things that you feel passionate about. Appreciate all that you do well. Thoughts of not being good enough are just that, thoughts. They are misperceptions that were probably fed to you by someone else, and you can release them starting right now. Set yourself up for success.

Old: I am ugly.
New: I am beautiful.

Imagine seeing yourself as God sees you. Learn to appreciate your looks and the miracle of your body. True beauty comes from within, which shines through when you show the world who you really are.

Old: I am a failure.
New: I am a success.

Every mistake offers you a chance to see the light and to learn from the mistake. Bless these mistakes, and see them as golden opportunities that gift you with wisdom and awareness and prompt you to choose again. Sometimes our worst "failures" propel us toward our greatest successes. So, look for the silver lining, bless the lessons, and forgive yourself if you need to. Take heed of Thomas Edison's words, "Our greatest weakness lies in giving up. The most certain way to succeed is always to try just one more time."

Old: I am in debt.
New: I am financially abundant.

Concentrate on $100, $1,000, or whatever you have at any given time, and appreciate that money. Send love out, and bless rich people. Don't compare what you have to what others have. Release thoughts of jealousy and envy and of being undeserving. Fully imagine your wealthy self.

Old: I am stupid.
New: I am intelligent.

Every mind is a miracle. Some of us shine academically, some shine with street smarts, some shine creatively—every mind shines in its own way. When you connect with Divine intelligence, you have all the smarts you could possibly desire.

Old: I feel old.
New: I feel youthful, and my body feels great.

Your thoughts regarding age and health, about yourself as well as others, greatly determine how young and good you feel. Appreciate everything that does look and feel good and find beneficial activities you can partake in that support wellness. Be proactive in preventative health. Change your beliefs about age and health, and choose to slow the aging process.

Old: Nobody likes me.
New: I am well liked and respected.

Your thoughts mirror your reality, and if you don't think highly enough of yourself, those you attract in your life will reflect that. Choose to be happy, and seek out activities that make you feel joyful. Learn to enjoy your own company. You are loved beyond measure, and as you learn to like and love yourself, you will attract others who feel the same about you.

Old: I am not creative.
New: I am a highly creative being.

Just being human is a very creative act. Creativity isn't limited to the act of putting something on paper or canvas, writing a song, or designing a building. We are creative in how we communicate with others, how we choose to spend our days, and how we help ourselves, and others, to have better lives. We all have individual creative talents, and when we recognize and honor them, we breed even more creativity.

Old: I am weird.
New: I am wonderfully unique.

How boring would life be if everyone had the same "normal" personality? Many of us feel weird and do not fit in, but that is not a bad thing. Living outside the box makes you a unique individual, perhaps one that will help create a better world. By the way, what is weird now may be the norm one day. But who cares? Just be who you really are, and be content.

Old: I am powerless.
New: I am powerful beyond belief.

We are all powerful spiritual beings, as we all create our realities. What is more powerful than that? We need to tap into that power, release any fears around it, and own who we really are.

Old: I am lazy.
New: I am energetic.

We are often lazy when we aren't living in our passion. Find what excites you most, and simply do it! You can start small and commit a portion of your free time to this activity. Soon you'll find that you have energy you didn't realize you had, which then allows you to move further into your passion. Sometimes we are lazy and need to be, especially as we continue to raise our vibrations and must rest our bodies to keep up.

Old: I am unlucky.
New: I create my own luck.

When we release ourselves from the prison of victimhood and own our true power, we find that luck is not randomly bestowed upon us—we don't passively receive it—we create it. Align your thoughts, feelings, words, and actions with success.

Old: I put everyone's needs before my own.
New: When I put myself first, everyone wins.

We need to nurture ourselves first. This will allow us to be the best we can be for others. Otherwise, we exhaust ourselves by serving our loved ones, in particular, and then what do we have left to give? Do everyone a favor, most of all yourself, and move toward taking better care of yourself. If you're not used to nurturing your own self, you may have to start small. Soon you will see the larger picture and give yourself permission to take better care of you.

Old: I feel alone.
New: I feel love and connection.

You are never alone. Start by acknowledging Divine presence in your life and by feeling unconditional love from God and your angels. Learn to love yourself as you are loved. Then you will attract others who will desire your company and love you as well. Many people suffer from loneliness, and the Universe will bring people together when the new thoughts are in line with love and connection. This often requires the action of being out in the world and meeting people.

Old: I am a smoker.
New: I choose excellent health.

Release the thoughts and verbal identifications of being a *smoker* from your daily existence. As you attract the best way to cease this habit, concentrate on the end result: one who chooses excellent health.

Old: I am fat.
New: I am healthy, and I look and feel great.

Release the thoughts and verbal identifications of being an *overweight* person from your daily existence. As you attract the best plan to gain health, keep imagining yourself as having the shape you desire. Focus on the end result—improved health, looking and feeling fabulous, moving well, and being more active.

Old: I am hurting.
New: I am the master of my emotions.

Once you know how you create your reality, you learn to master your life and your emotions. Your pain doesn't have the same charge, because you see things from a higher perspective. Feelings are the language of the soul, and you must honor all feelings, of course, but you then learn what is behind the hurt and acquire a higher understanding and a healthy perspective.

Old: I am bored.
New: I am excited.

Nothing about life is boring when you really open your eyes, especially when you open up spiritually. You are bored because you haven't stepped into your passion and life itself. Start by nurturing yourself and finding things to get excited about. Open your mind to the possibilities. Intend to discover your own unique path, and soon you will wake up excited to begin each day.

Old: I am nothing.
New: I am important.

Everyone is important. The best way to "choose again" with this misbelief is to serve others in some way. Gandhi said, "The best way to find yourself is to lose yourself in the service of others." What would you think of a man who'd felt he led an unsuccessful life, never living up to his potential, but who then in his seventies volunteered to help abused children? He becomes a mentor for dozens of kids and touches their lives, providing hope, love, and healing. Every single person has something special to give and do.

Old: I am phony.
New: I am real.

Relationships serve as our best mirrors. You will attract those who will in some way tell you that you aren't being your true self or who will mirror that same quality so that you can see yourself in them. If you practice being a more authentic individual and celebrate who you really are, you will be most content.

Old: I am weak.
New: I am strong.

As you learn to own who you really are—a powerful spiritual being—the human traits of vulnerability and helplessness lessen. Weakness is merely an illusion.

Old: I don't deserve what I want.
New: I fully deserve what I desire.

No matter how much you want something, if, deep down, you don't feel you deserve it, you will have a hard time attracting it. If you somehow do, you may not allow yourself to enjoy it, or it will perhaps disappear in time. God wants us to be happy and to manifest what we wish for in our lives. Simply change your mind if you want to easily attract and enjoy whatever you desire.

Old: I'll never achieve greatness.
New: I am achieving greatness.

Some of us compare ourselves to famous people and tell ourselves that we couldn't ever be that talented, smart, innovative, charismatic, beautiful, handsome, or rich. Well, you don't have to be famous to achieve greatness. Your greatness may or may not be in the limelight. What does greatness really mean to you? Acknowledge all the ways that you shine.

Old: I don't trust people.
New: I surround myself with trustworthy people.

The belief that people cannot be trusted will attract those who match that belief, people who cannot be trusted. Use your imagination to see yourself socializing with, working with, and coming into contact with trustworthy people. Release your worries, and instead count on your built-in intuition and discernment to affirm those whom you can trust.

Old: People drive me nuts.
New: I am grateful for the wonderful people in my life.

The focus on people driving you nuts will attract more of the same, people whom you don't want to be around. When you are grateful for those in your life who are wonderful and for the positive qualities they possess, even if it's just one or two friends or family members, you will attract new relationships with more wonderful people. When relationships challenge you from time to time, as they do for all of us, recognize the gifts of their mirrors, which contribute to your self-awareness and personal growth.

Old: I am flawed.
New: I am perfect just as I am.

Remember that every human being has flaws, but we cannot allow them to stop us from achieving our greatest successes. Think more in terms of tapping into your endless potential. "If we did all the things we are capable of, we would literally astound ourselves," said Thomas Edison. As you focus on your shining abilities, your attention on your flaws will melt away. You are perfect just as you are.

Old: Life is a drag.
New: Life is a gift.

If you believe that life is a drag, you lack appreciation and thus prevent the flow of wonderful things to grace your life. Seek out those things that bring you joy, and feel that joy on a deep level. It's never too late to change your perceptions. Infuse your life with humor—watch funny movies, share jokes, or place your favorite cartoons on your bathroom mirror—which will help you to maintain a light and jovial attitude. When challenges appear, as they do for everyone, see how they can propel your growth. Allow your blessed self to be in awe of life's infinite gifts, no matter what their disguise.

Old: Life is a struggle.
New: I live life easily and effortlessly.

Create a mantra, whenever you are involved with any activity, event, issue, project, or relationship that used to attract struggle, and say, "_____ comes easily and effortlessly." Imagine paying off debt, making an important decision with your spouse, settling a difference at work, and doing chores around the house, all with a sense of ease. Also, you can just say the words "easy and effortless" as many times a day as you can to retrain your subconscious with the new desired perception. Of course, life throws curves to us, and because we are human, we do experience complications so that we can learn from them; however, we can intend to have less struggle in our lives while still accomplishing our lessons. Our attitude is everything.

Old: Pain follows pleasure.
New: Pleasure follows pleasure.

Sometimes it's hard for some of us to be happy. For one, if things are going well, we may feel that something bad will soon come to ruin it all. This is a common misbelief. Even though pain is sometimes a part of life, don't you want to attract as much pleasure as you possibly can? Choose to believe that pleasure follows pleasure and even more pleasure.

Old: There is not enough.
New: There is more than enough.

See your life from the perspective of abundance rather than lack. Intend to tap into our wildly abundant Universe, with your appropriate thoughts, feelings, words, and actions. Lack is only your misperception. Change your beliefs and behavior, and you will find yourself with more than enough.

Old: Life is too easy; life is just routine (all birth scripts).
New: (Choose a supportive replacement of the nonsupportive belief acquired at birth.)

No matter what misbeliefs you may have acquired at birth because of the type of birthing you experienced—and these may remain in your subconscious mind, as described in the chapter "A New Way of Living"—you can release these misbeliefs. Then consciously choose the appropriate new belief and any necessary supportive actions.

It bears repeating that the misbeliefs mentioned above are often miraculously mirrored through relationships. So, if you are unaware of what your negative self-thoughts are (we all have them to varying degrees), as most are acquired from our childhoods and past lives, look at what goes on with your mate, your friends, your family, your co-workers, and absolute strangers. Is there something that really bugs you about them? Is it that they are weak? Are they taking advantage of you? Are they fearful? Are they failing? Are they hurtful? Are they boring? Are they manipulative? Are they hard to love?

Whatever qualities they possess that you find irritating could be valuable gifts in disguise. They may, and I stress the word *may*, be mirroring what you don't like about yourself on a deep level. Once you honestly connect with this awareness, you can concentrate on your own healing and choose again. When you do, you will probably find that there is no longer the same charge. They may not frustrate you as much, and, in fact, they may change as well.

Because our relationships offer the greatest opportunities for healing, if you aren't allowing yourself the awareness of what is truly going on behind the scenes, then synchronicity and the Law of Attraction will continue to mirror it for you, perhaps with new and more faces until you get it.

As you heal yourself and choose again, remember to get your feelings behind the new thoughts and actions. Pay attention to the words you speak and make sure they are in alignment. Take ownership of the positive beliefs, knowing that you have the full support of God and the angels. Always choose love—love for yourself and for others—and all will be well.

CHAPTER 21

ASK YOUR ANGELS FOR A
MESSAGE

*T*he following meditation will allow you to achieve a heightened state of awareness so that you can easily receive a direct message from your angels. This can be an extremely powerful tool to gain validation or direction in your life. It will awaken you to the higher dimensions and help you see things clearly, even something well beyond your expectations. Therefore, you need to be open and allow for the information to come forth. My clients and students have considered this to be an exciting method of attaining valuable knowledge and have often found it life-altering as well.

I recommend that you either tape yourself slowly reading the following script and then play it back to yourself or ask a trusted friend or family member to read it live, without interruption, and perhaps while playing soft, meditative music. Of course, meditations must occur only when you are fully inactive and in the quiet of your own personal space, most certainly not while driving. Information about attaining this meditation on CD can be found in the back of this book.

*   *   *   *

Close your eyes, and take a very deep breath in, breathing in peace …
and exhaling tension … another deep breath in with peace … and out
with the release of all tension … and one more in with peace … and out
with anything unlike peace. Perfect … Now, begin to relax your whole
body, starting at the crown of your head and breathing peace and relaxation into any part that feels tense. Feel every muscle in your face relax:
your eyes, your cheeks, and your jaw are completely limp and loose; your
teeth are slightly parted; your neck, arms, and hands are all fully relaxed.
Release all tension in your chest, your abdomen, the whole length of your
back, your hips, and buttocks. Deeply relax all these areas. Relax your legs
all the way down to your toes, feeling so completely relaxed. Check to
make sure you are feeling totally calm and peaceful. Just scan your body
and breathe relaxation into any place that may still hold tension. (pause)
Now relax your mind, and if any unwelcome thoughts come, say, "Thank
you for sharing," and then just let them drift away. (pause)

Now imagine before you a beautiful white stone staircase with seven
steps going upward. In a moment, you will slowly go up the staircase, and
with each step, you will feel a sense of greater awareness. Look up to see
the Divine white light shining from above that will soon fill you with great
peace, love, comfort, and healing energy. When you reach the top of the
staircase, an angelic presence will be there to greet you. Now go ahead and
take the first step up, feeling the light starting to come down through the
crown of your head, this Divine white healing light. Step two—the warm
light comes down, down through your body. It is shining healing energy
anywhere you intend it—your head, your neck, your heart, your back—
wherever you wish, as it continues down your body and out your hands
and feet. (pause) Step three—it's an endless supply, this beautiful light,
and you can call it forth any time. You feel even more deeply relaxed as
this loving and healing light fills every part of your body, every cell, every
bone, every muscle, tissue, and organ—every fiber of your being. (pause)
Step four—you become aware of an angelic presence waiting for you at the
top of the stairs, a high being coming only from the light. Step five—you
feel gratitude for this being's presence and look forward to the gift of a
message. Step six—you continue to feel the light coming through your

crown and out your hands and feet. You're so close to the angel now. Step seven, seven, seven—you're at the top of the stairs, and you greet this beautiful being. (pause) What does your angel look like? (pause) Do you recognize him or her? (pause) Ask your angel what his or her name is. (pause) If you don't hear anything, that is fine, too.

Now ask what message this angel has for you and then listen for the answer. (long pause) If you did not receive a message, it may come in some form at another time. All is perfect as is.

Now ask your angel any specific questions you have for guidance or validation. (long pause)

Now ask your angel for help in any area of your life. (long pause)

When the experience of being together feels complete for now, thank your angel, expressing your heartfelt appreciation for his or her love and guidance. You may choose to ask your angel to meet you again at the top of the stairs at some future time. (pause)

You are still feeling the light coming from above, flowing through your body, out your hands and feet, down into the earth; this unconditional Divine love and healing light stays with you long after this meditation. If you are listening to this just prior to going to sleep, go ahead and drift off into a wonderfully peaceful, restful sleep. Otherwise, when the time feels right, go ahead and open your eyes and return to the outside world.

∗   ∗   ∗   ∗

In order to ground yourself following this meditation, you may wish to move your feet back and forth on the floor, drink some water, walk around, or get some fresh air. Make sure you are fully alert before you continue on with your day.

I hope this meditation has gifted you with awareness, transformation, and healing. You can ask your angels for additional help or clarity. If you didn't receive any messages, you may need to be patient for them to come forth in a different way. It may come through your dreams, for instance, as dreams give you the opportunity to explore your inner world and show you some of your most vivid signs. Maybe it will come through the wise words of the next person you speak to or on a future visit at the top of the stairs. Allow yourself to trust the process. The Universe, your angels, will bring you the awareness you desire. Just be open and allow.

CHAPTER 22

LIVING A SYNCHRONISTIC LIFESTYLE

Synchronicity is God winking at us. When we notice it, we are winking right back. When we grow our awareness of the miracles of everyday living, our connection with God builds, we feel gratitude for the guidance and gifts, and we naturally become co-creators and consciously create the lives we desire. We simply live in sync with God.

After twelve years of living with a grand awareness of synchronicity, I have developed a list of ways for you to assimilate this gift into everyday life. The actions described in this list are not meant to be memorized or rigidly followed, as they come naturally once you attain awareness and intend to live in this manner. Thus, I offer the following as a guideline only; it is merely a list of suggestions to keep in mind. These qualities will easily and effortlessly appear when you make the choice to live a synchronistic lifestyle.

- *Act more like a willow than an oak*—be especially flexible when deciphering meanings of signs.

- *Allow for joyful, even ecstatic states*—you would expect everyone to want this, but we do so only when we grow tired of perpetuating our own dramas and ultimately choose fulfillment.

- *Awaken and utilize your intuition*—your intuition is a form of knowledge that provides wisdom. It can come through images, sensations, smells, sounds, and flashes of inner knowingness—we all process differently. We are all naturally intuitive but may not be picking up on it or trusting it.

- *Be open to messages from the Heavenly realms*—unusual and unexpected things may occur when angels are trying to get your attention. Your openness can attract precious Heavenly gifts into your human experience.

- *Bless each sign, whether good or bad*—see things from a higher perspective, and bless each message no matter how bad it may seem.

- *Express constant and heartfelt gratitude*—for God, synchronicities, your angels, and all the blessings in your life.

- *Go with the flow*—an unexpected occurrence or an uninvited inconvenience may be a blessing in disguise, as it may provide a new opportunity or a chance for synchronicity to express itself. Let go and let God.

- *Have a willingness to explore*—be a pioneer as a "synchronist," walking the exciting path of conscious co-creation through the use of synchronicities and discovering uncharted territory by connecting to the Heavenly realms as a human being.

- *Increase your awareness of everything*—what are the lyrics of a song telling you? What words did you overhear when sitting in the restaurant? What was the message of your dream? Who are you meeting by chance, and what message do they have for you or do you have for them? What is the cloud shape in the sky validating or guiding you to do? How is nature constantly speaking to you? The better you understand that the Universe is guiding, validating, and illuminating your life, the more you become *relentlessly* aware of the messages.

- *Keep an open mind*—very important! At times you may feel out of your mind, beyond conventional thinking, and that is actually the desired process. When you allow yourself to see from outside the box, you'll attract more "aha" moments by making the necessary connections.

- *Live creatively*—synchronistic living is a highly creative act. Be especially creative in your awareness, your thoughts and imagination, your deciphering of meanings of signs, your relationships with angels, and your new choices for conscious creation.

- *Maintain a playful attitude*—have great fun with signs. To me, there is nothing more fun than living synchronistically and embracing your inner child. See things as simply as a child would, without attachment and fears that we adults often create.

- *Match your thoughts, feelings, words, and actions with your greatest desires*—extremely important! What you think, feel, say, and do manifests—it's the Law of Attraction. If you are feeling negative, everything is going to manifest that way, including your attraction of negative synchronicity. When your thoughts, feelings, words, and actions are in line with your desires, you synchronistically create the life you really want.

- *Respect the serious business of signs*—they can save your life or prevent hardship. If you're somehow getting the message to go back home and check to make sure you turned off the stove, for example, follow the sign.

- *Seek and acknowledge the positive in the negative*—that is part of mastering life!

- *Show trust but always balance with caution*—it's very important to always use discernment.

- *Understand that subconscious memories sometimes need to be brought up and released*—synchronicity reflects your subconscious as well as conscious mind, so you bless what comes up, even when painful, and then release the negative effects of these memories for good.

Remember, your thoughts, feelings, words, and actions are creating not only your life but also your synchronistic life. If you are drowning in your own fears, synchronicity will show you signs that reflect those fears. When you let go of the fears and adopt a more positive outlook, the messages will mirror your new, more optimistic beliefs. So, you need to make sure you are operating increasingly out of love and less out of fear—a most critical part of the spiritual path. Less fear means more trust in God.

*   *   *   *

There you have it. Synchronicity really does happen. So spread the word. Spread your excitement. Share your experiences, and let them ripple out into eternity. What a gift that is for others. Perhaps one day it will be in vogue to recognize the magic of signs.

Embrace the synchronicity that is occurring in your life. Approach your understanding in a childlike manner, and get excited. When you share it with others, be playful with it. Tap into your God-given intuition, your inner wisdom, with confidence. Allow yourself to fully benefit from the guidance or validation that the synchronicity provides, and show gratitude for it; your gratitude will only attract more.

Laugh and scream with joy when you see 444, when a wild animal shows you the way, when a song courts you with the perfect words you need to hear, when a cloud's shape brings you to tears, when water rains on your abundant self, and when a stranger comes out of nowhere and becomes your perfect mirror. And feel God's grace touch you so profoundly that you fall down on your knees.

As you grow in awareness of the gift of synchronicity, you will naturally see life more clearly. You become fully conscious of who you really are and why you are here. Signs will illuminate any obstacles in your way. Fear dissolves as more light shines. Your days become so much brighter, with ever-blue skies.

My heartfelt prayer is that this book has succeeded in expressing how God, through synchronicity, is constantly blessing all of us with miracles, beautifully illuminating the powerful, creative, intuitive, and Divine beings that we are. May you bask in the light of this most grand awareness. May you internalize this gift, breathing it into every cell of your being. May you clearly see God's constant presence in every area of your life. May you tap into the depths of who you really are and recognize your infinite potential. May your enlightened presence gently, yet powerfully, inspire others. And may we together manifest a more peaceful, healthy, and loving earth, the one we are destined to create.

Afterword

My experiences shared in this book occurred in my life because of only one reason. Each time, I surrendered to God's messages, through that incredible mirror He uses—synchronicity. Had I not opened my eyes to see clearly, I would not have noticed that my life was being fully illuminated. I would not have saved that Chihuahua. I would not have even gotten into my car to allow the German shepherd and the perfect words to teach me my grandest lesson of unconditional love and forgiveness. I would care less about numbers. I would have failed to find any personal meaning in lyrics through the many song synchronicities that have so brightened my life. I would not have found myself in that hotel gift shop to receive a message that would profoundly change me forever. I would have dismissed the numerous Molly and rose synchronicities as purely coincidence and certainly would not have discovered a most significant message about our future and our salvation. And, well, obviously, you would not have just read this book.

Bibliography

Bach, Richard. *Illusions: The Adventures of a Reluctant Messiah.* New York: Dell Publishing, 1994.

Brown, Dan. *The Da Vinci Code.* New York: Doubleday, 2003.

Bunick, Nick. *In God's Truth.* Charlottesville: Hampton Roads, 1998.

Carroll, Lee. *Kryon.* Del Mar: The Kryon Writings. The Kryon books, 1993–2007. Eleven numbered volumes.

Coelho, Paulo. *Eleven Minutes.* New York: HarperCollins, 2004.

Eker, Harv T. *Secrets of the Millionaire Mind: Mastering the Inner Game of Wealth.* New York: HarperCollins, 2005.

Emoto, Masaru. *Messages from Water.* Tokyo: HADO Kyoikusha, 1999.

Gaffney, Patricia. *The Saving Graces.* New York: Harpertorch, 1999.

Gawain, Shakti. *Living in the Light.* Rev. ed. Novato: Nataraj Publishing, 1998.

Hawkins, David R. *Power vs. Force: The Hidden Determinants of Human Behavior.* Carlsbad: Hay House, 2002.

Hicks, Esther, and Jerry. *The Law of Attraction: The Basics of the Teachings of Abraham.* Carlsbad: Hay House, 2006.

Ingram, Julia, and G. W. Hardin. *The Messengers: A True Story of Angelic Presence and the Return to the Age of Miracles*. New York: Pocket Books, 1996.

Jung, C. G. *Synchronicity: An Acausal Connecting Principle*, trans. R. F. C. Hull. 2nd ed. Princeton: Princeton University Press, 1969.

Linn, Denise. *The Secret Language of Signs: How to Interpret the Coincidences and Symbols in Your Life*. New York: Ballantine Books, 1996.

Milanovich, Norma, and Shirley McCune. *The Light Shall Set You Free*. Albuquerque: Athena Publishing, 1996.

Millman, Dan. *The Life You Were Born to Live: A Guide to Finding Your Life Purpose*. Tiburon: H. J. Kramer, 1993.

Ovason, David. *Prophecies for America*. New York: Avon, 2001.

Redfield, James. *The Celestine Prophecy: An Adventure*. New York: Warner Books, 1993.

Rowling, J. K. *Harry Potter and the Sorcerer's Stone*. New York: Scholastic, 1997.

Virtue, Doreen. *Angel Visions*. Carlsbad: Hay House, 2000.

Virtue, Doreen. *Archangels & Ascended Masters*. Carlsbad: Hay House, 2003.

Walsch, Neale Donald. *Conversations with God: an uncommon dialogue*. New York: Putnam, 1995.

Ward, Suzanne. *Matthew, Tell Me About Heaven: A Firsthand Description of the Afterlife*. Rev. ed. Camas: Matthew Publishers, 2002.

Weiss, Brian L. *Many Lives, Many Masters*. New York: Fireside, 1988.

Weiss, Brian L. *Only Love Is Real*. New York: Warner Books, 1996.

Williamson, Marianne. *A Return to Love*. New York: HarperCollins, 1993.

American Heritage Dictionary of the English Language, 4th ed., s. v. "synchronicity," http://dictionary.reference.com/browse/synchronicity (accessed July 10, 2007).

Dictionary.com Unabridged (v. 1.1), s. v. "coincidence," http://dictionary.reference.com/browse/coincidence (accessed July 10, 2007).

Can You See Clearly Now?

Have you experienced an amazing synchronicity that you wish to share with others? If you would like to have it considered for inclusion in my future book detailing miraculous, inspiring, and life-transforming synchronicities, please e-mail your typed story (up to 2,000 words) to mary@marysoliel.com, or send it to:

Mary Soliel
A Lighthouse in the Rockies, LLC
PO Box 822
Louisville, CO 80027 U.S.A.

Be sure to include your name, address, phone number, and e-mail address, and you will be promptly notified of receipt of your submission. Please save a copy, because story submissions will not be returned. Also, know that publishing a book can be a lengthy process. I greatly thank you in advance for your contribution, which will help illuminate the miracles that grace our world.

Ask Your Angels for a Message
CD Offer

To order your copy of *Ask Your Angels for a Message* CD, a gently guided meditation by Mary Soliel, please send your shipping information and $17 for each CD in U.S. Funds only (add $3 for S&H—outside the United States or Canada add $5) to:

A Lighthouse in the Rockies, LLC
PO Box 822
Louisville, CO 80027 U.S.A.

Visit www.marysoliel.com to find out about other meditation CDs available.

978-0-595-45860-8
0-595-45860-2

p. 34 - # meanings

Lightning Source UK Ltd.
Milton Keynes UK
174195UK00002B/97/P